OSPREY AVIATION ELITE • 3

No 91 'Nigeria' Squadron

SERIES EDITOR: TONY HOLMES

OSPREY AVIATION ELITE • 3

No 91 'Nigeria' Squadron

Peter Hall

OSPREY
AVIATION

Front cover
Late in the evening of 25 May 1943, four No 91 Sqn Spitfire XIIs were scrambled to intercept an estimated 15 Fw 190A-5s that had been detected by coastal radar heading for Folkestone. These aircraft almost certainly hailed from *Schnellkampf-geschwader* 10, which had been carrying out dusk and night-bombing attacks on coastal towns in the south-east of England since mid April. Often arriving over their targets at great speed totally unannounced, the German pilots had caused considerable damage and loss of life during the campaign to date, but on this occasion they more than met their match. The Intelligence Form 'F' of No 91 Sqn's CO, Sqn Ldr Raymond Harries, describes what happened next;

'I was leading Blue section, comprising four aircraft of No 91 Sqn, on a defensive patrol. I had just returned to base, and with my No 2 had just landed when the scramble signal was given from the watch office. We both immediately took off again, and saw enemy aircraft approaching Folkestone.

'I immediately dived towards the sea, the enemy aircraft turning back and jettisoning their bombs immediately they saw us. Going over Folkestone I experienced very heavy flak, luckily inaccurate, from our ground defences. I sighted one lone FW190 at sea level returning to France. I came in from his starboard side, delivering a three-second burst at 250 yards. Enemy aircraft hit the sea tail first, split in two and sank immediately.

'I then spotted another FW190 to starboard. I flew straight over the top of it in order to identify it in the failing light. Enemy aircraft pulled up his nose and gave me a quick squirt. I pulled straight up to about 1000 ft, and turning to port, dived right on to his tail, opening fire from 300 yards and closing to 150 yards. I fired a four-second burst, seeing strikes and flashes all over the enemy aircraft. Enemy aircraft lost height very gradually, with smoke and flames coming from it, skimmed for some distance along the surface of the water and then sank. This was confirmed by Flt Lt Matthew and Flt Lt Kynaston. I orbited around taking cine gun snaps of the oil patch and pieces of wreckage that were visible' (*Cover artwork by Jim Laurier*)

Dedication
For Lynne Corder, who possesses the same fighting spirit as those featured in this book. They would have liked her.

First published in Great Britain in 2001 by Osprey Publishing
Elms Court, Chapel Way, Botley, Oxford, OX2 9LP
E-mail: info@ospreypublishing.com

ISBN 1 84176 160 5

Edited by Tony Holmes
Page design by Mark Holt
Cover Artwork by Jim Laurier
Aircraft Profiles by Chris Davey
Photo Captions by Peter Hall and Tony Holmes
Origination by Grasmere Digital Imaging, Leeds, UK
Printed through Bookbuilders, Hong Kong

01 02 03 04 10 9 8 7 6 5 4 3 2 1

ACKNOWLEDGEMENTS
The Editor wishes to express his thanks to Roy Humphreys, Philip Jarrett, Andy Saunders and Andy Thomas for the provision of photographs included within this volume.

EDITOR'S NOTE
To make this new series as authoritative as possible, the Editor would be interested in hearing from any individual who may have relevant photographs, documentation or first-hand experiences relating to aircrews, and their aircraft, of the various theatres of war. Any material used will be credited to its original source. Please write to Tony Holmes at 10 Prospect Road, Sevenoaks, Kent, TN13 3UA, Great Britain, or by e-mail at: tony.holmes@osprey-jets.freeserve.co.uk

CONTENTS

INTRODUCTION

I first became aware of the exploits of No 91 Sqn whilst researching a history of RAF West Malling, in Kent. From its humble beginnings as a reconnaissance flight, using 'second-hand' aircraft at the very end of the Battle of Britain, the 'Jim Crow' squadron went on to become one of the most famous, and successful, units in Fighter Command.

No 91 Sqn's forerunner, No 421 Flt, was born of necessity when the RAF was probably at its weakest, being short of both pilots and aircraft. Despite this, throughout its brief but hectic history, both the flight and the squadron excelled at whatever types of operation were thrust its way. The appearance of the Bf 109F and the Fw 190 on the western front caused the squadron real problems, for both fighter types were superior to the unit's early-model Spitfires, yet its pilots fought on and achieved victories with the odds heavily stacked against them.

Unlike other fighter units, No 91 Sqn flew operations in single aircraft strength from its earliest days, resulting in its pilots often fighting – and dying – alone. These operations fostered an entirely different breed of fighter pilot – a determined individualist who did not always fit in when posted to other squadrons! The unit was also unusual in that it had a wide range of nationalities serving on it throughout the war. None wanted to leave when their own national squadrons were formed, and a least one that did leave soon returned.

The determination to succeed against an often technically superior enemy, the outstanding achievements in the air and the legendary squadron spirit which enabled pilots and groundcrews to enjoy memorable social evenings together on the ground, have earned No 91 Sqn its place in RAF history – it should not be forgotten.

Any study of an RAF fighter squadron in the war years would not be complete without reference to the superb *Aces High* (Grub Street, 1994), written by Christopher Shores and Clive Williams, and its sequel, *Aces High Volume 2* (Grub Street 1999), again by Christopher Shores. It was a privilege to help with No 91 Sqn's 'Diver' claims for the latter volume, and the importance of both books to the aviation historian cannot be overstated.

Throughout this book I have used Combat Reports and other contemporary material, much of it reproduced verbatim. The grammar, punctuation and terms used are those common at the time, and these may seem strange 60 years later!

Peter Hall
Ashford
January 2001

EARLY DAYS

October 1940. The long hot summer had faded into autumn, and what became known as the Battle of Britain was almost over. The Luftwaffe had largely abandoned its highly successful attacks on RAF airfields and switched instead to striking at London and other cities, firstly by day and then by night. The change in German tactics was crucial to Fighter Command. It gave Air Chief-Marshal Sir Hugh Dowding a chance to rest his worn out pilots, repair his airfields and build up his stocks of aircraft, whilst RAF nightfighters attempted to counter the *Blitz*.

The Luftwaffe was far from being a spent force, however, and continued, albeit on a reduced scale, to attack the air force in the air and on the ground. It was therefore essential that during Fighter Command's rest and reformation period, no time or resources were wasted on fruitless patrols. The excellent Chain Home radar system was invaluable in this, but in order to enhance the radar information, another source of intelligence was required.

A plan was devised whereby one, or perhaps two, fighter aircraft would patrol the coast and over the English Channel at high altitude. Their task was specifically to report on movements of enemy aircraft, and the tactics they adopted in combat. These types of operations were code-named 'Jim Crows' – inspired by a cartoon character of a bad-tempered crow, wearing a top hat and carrying an umbrella!

On 8 October 1940 No 421 Flt was formed at RAF Gravesend, in Kent, as a detached flight of No 66 Sqn. The role of the flight was to maintain patrols over the Channel, and report on the movements of enemy aircraft – they were the first 'Jim Crow' unit. The flight was equipped with six Spitfire IIAs, which also came from No 66 Sqn, and was commanded by ex-No 92 Sqn flight commander, Flt Lt C P 'Paddy' Green. The original pilots were:

Flg Off J J O'Meara	Sgt D H Forrest
Flg Off H C Baker	Sgt A W P Spears
Flg Off P McD Hartas	Sgt C A H Ayling
Plt Off K A Lawrence	Sgt M A W Lee
Flt Sgt J Gillies	

(Flt Lt J Saunders assisted with the formation of the flight and then left)

This fuzzy snap taken at Hawkinge in November 1940 is possibly the only photograph in existence to show a No 421 Flt aircraft – in this case Spitfire IIA P7531. The fighter was flown on a number of occasions by the flight's OC, Flt Lt Charles 'Paddy' Green (11 destroyed, 3 and 1 shared probable and 1 damaged). Initially delivered to the RAF in late October 1940, Spitfire IIA P7531 spent a week with RAE Farnborough on diving trials, where the degree of tail deflection needed to cope with various loads was measured. Restored to standard configuration, the fighter was issued to No 421 Flt on 8 November 1940. It continued to serve with No 91 Sqn until it was shot down off Ostend by Unteroffizier Amhausend of I./JG 2 on 24 April 1941. Its pilot, Plt Off Peall, bailed out and was rescued by the Margate lifeboat (*via Roy Humphreys*)

The flight managed two short patrols on its first day in existence, and there was to be no rest for its pilots, many of whom had fought throughout the summer months. The air battles were still raging over southern England and, for the time being, these took precedence over 'Jim Crows'.

Thus, No 421 Flt found itself initially employed as a standard day fighter unit, and on 10 October Sgt Lee force-landed his Spitfire at Gravesend after it had been damaged by cannon fire during combat with Bf 109s. The flight suffered its first casualty when Sgt Charles Ayling was shot down and killed (in Spitfire P7303) at 1600 hrs whilst patrolling near Newchurch, in Kent. Twenty-eight-year-old Ayling had been a pre-war sergeant pilot with No 43 Sqn, seeing action with the Hurricane unit in France, as well as throughout the summer months. Joining No 66 Sqn in September, he had transferred to No 421 Flt just weeks later.

On 12 October the flight was completely re-equipped with Hurricane IIAs, thus becoming the first frontline unit to receive the latest mark of Hawker fighter – although it managed to keep two Spitfire IIAs. And it was whilst flying one of the latter fighters (P7441) on the 12th that Flt Lt Green suffered an iced up cockpit when shadowing a formation of enemy aircraft at 30,000 ft.

Whilst temporarily 'blind', he was 'bounced' by Bf 109Es of JG 52 and his controls shot away. Green was wounded in the neck and arm, and he struggled to open the cockpit hood as the Spitfire fell from 30,000 to 1000 ft. At 700 ft he finally bailed out and was picked up by New Zealand soldiers, his aircraft, meanwhile, having crashed and burned out at Coldbridge, near Boughton Malherbe.

After losing three Spitfires in two days without as much as having even damaged a Luftwaffe aircraft, the pilots of No 421 Flt at last 'broke their duck' on 15 October when Sgt Lee used Spitfire IIA P7444 to down a Bf 109E whilst patrolling at 27,000 ft south of Maidstone. However, his aircraft was badly damaged in a later attack during the same sortie, and then wrecked in an attempted forced-landing at Blackham Farm, Broadoak, near Canterbury. Sgt Lee was admitted to hospital with slight wounds, although he returned to the flight soon afterwards. Another No 421 Flt Spitfire carried out a forced-landing that same day when a newly-arrived replacement fighter suffered an engine failure whilst being flown by New Zealander Plt Off Keith Lawrence.

No 66 Sqn moved from Gravesend to RAF West Malling on 31 October, and No 421 Flt went with it. West Malling was still under construction at this time, and both units operated from the old Maidstone Airport building in the north-west corner of the Kentish airfield. The flight undertook its first sorties from the station on 1 November and, much to the delight of everyone, ex-No 41 Sqn pilot (and future ace) Flg Off Henry Baker destroyed a Bf 109 and probably downed another whilst at the controls of a Hurricane. His Combat Report tells the story:

'While doing a spotting patrol over the coast I sighted nine Me109s at 25,000 ft. Following them, I gave a few bursts totalling three seconds up into the formation with no visible effect. I then lost sight of them, but shortly afterwards at 1430 hrs approximately, I saw bombs falling in the sea about 20 miles north-east of Margate. Above, at about 5000 ft, I saw about 40 Me109s in two groups of about 20, and 12 vics of three Do17s, which were milling around and apparently attacking shipping. I first

Flt Lt 'Paddy' Green poses with his Husky and his shotgun at Hawkinge in the weak winter sun on New Year's Day 1941. It is difficult to tell whether the bags under his eyes were caused by the endless daily cycle of fighter-recce missions, or the memorable new year's party held in the officers' mess the previous night!

A most capable leader of men, Charles Patrick 'Paddy' Green was a Cambridge University graduate, athletic 'Blue', Fellow of the Royal Geographic Society and British Four-Man Bobsleigh Team Bronze Medallist at the 1936 Winter Olympics. He was also a pre-war member of the Royal Auxiliary Air Force's No 601 'County of London' Sqn, known as the 'Millionaires' Mob' to the national press at the time. Called up upon the outbreak of war, Green was posted to No 92 Sqn in October 1939, and had been promoted to flight commander by early 1940. He claimed his first kill – a Bf 109E – over Dunkirk on 23 May, but was subsequently wounded just minutes later by a cannon shell fired from a Bf 110, which struck the cockpit of his Spitfire I (N3167) and caused a compound fracture of his right thigh.

Green remained off operations until posted to the newly-created No 421 Flt as its OC on 8 October 1940. He made three claims whilst with the unit, remaining in command after the flight became No 91 'Nigeria' Sqn in January 1941. Awarded a DFC in April, Green left the unit in June to fill the role of Squadron Leader Tactics with HQ, Fighter Command. In November he joined Beaufighter IIF-equipped No 600 Sqn as a flight commander, where he retrained as a nightfighter pilot. Given command of fellow nightfighting unit No 125 Sqn in June 1942, Green returned to No 600 Sqn in this capacity six months later. Now based in North Africa flying Beaufighter VIFs, he enjoyed great success over the next 12 months, claiming nine bombers shot down (including four Ju 88s in one night sortie over Sicily), two probably destroyed and one damaged.

Awarded a DSO in August 1943, 'Paddy' Green later commanded a wing of Boston bombers. He survived the war with the rank of group captain, and currently resides in Canada (*RAF Museum*)

made a beam attack into the belly of an Me109 which turned away. It was definitely hit, but I did not see what happened to it. I then sighted an Me109 which was pulling out from an attack on the water and gave him all the rest of my ammunition. I fired from above and behind him, and my burst went into the pilot's cockpit. The Me109 then went into a vertical dive and crashed into the sea.

'The Do17s carried normal camouflage, and the Me109s had yellow wing tips and yellow noses, with usual camouflage.

'Cloud 5/10ths at 25,000 ft, 4/10ths at 5000 ft. No cloud over sea.'

Bad weather prevented any further flying, and the flight moved from West Malling on 6 November. With No 66 Sqn, the unit had been posted to RAF Biggin Hill where, on the 9th, it was once again re-equipped with nine Spitfire IIAs thanks to the personal efforts of Flt Lt Green. The flight's stay at Kent's most famous fighter station was to be but a brief one, for No 11 Group HQ quickly realised it was pointless having a coastal reconnaissance unit based near London.

Thus, on 15 November, No 421 Flt finally separated from No 66 Sqn and moved to RAF Hawkinge, near Folkestone. Upon its arrival at the latter base it became the station's only resident unit, Hawkinge having until now seen extensive use as a forward airfield during the recent Battle of Britain. The move proved to be quite eventful, for ex-No 501 Sqn ace Sgt D A S 'Don' McKay (posted in on 22 October, having claimed six kills with his former unit) found a lone Do 17 near Folkestone. Flying Spitfire IIA P7499, he swiftly shot the bomber down into the sea, prior to landing at Hawkinge. McKay's victim was Do17Z-3 5K+FN of 5./KG 3.

Spitfire IIA P7490 *City of Coventry I* sits on the grass at No 66 Sqn's dispersal at Biggin Hill in early November 1940. Sharing 'LZ' codes with No 421 Flt (the latter unit had added a 'dash' between the 'L' and 'Z'), Fighter Command's second-oldest Spitfire squadron helped sire the specialist unit which eventually became No 91 Sqn. Aside from providing the flight with two experienced sergeant pilots, No 66 Sqn also equipped it with several Spitfire IIAs – although P7490 was not one of them. Delivered to No 9 Maintenance Unit (MU) straight from Vickers-Armstrongs' Castle Bromwich works on 2 October 1940, P7490 was the first of three consecutively-serialled Mk IIAs paid for by residents of Coventry. All issued to No 66 Sqn on 24 October, *City of Coventry II* (P7491) and *III* (P7492) were written off when they collided with each other during a patrol over Edenbridge on 28 November 1940 – 20-year-old Battle of Britain veteran Sgt P H Willcocks was killed in P7491, but future ace Flg Off Hubert 'Dizzy' Allen succeeded in bailing out of P7492. *City of Coventry I* enjoyed a much longer service career, however, seeing action with Nos 609, 65, 122 and 154 Sqns after leaving No 66 Sqn in late February 1941. Converted into a Spitfire ASR(IIC) in 1942, P7490 served with No 277 Air-Sea Rescue Sqn in 1943-44. And it is likely that it operated alongside No 91 Sqn from Hawkinge during this time. P7490 was Struck off Charge and sold for scrap later in 1944 (*via Phil Jarrett*)

Flt Lt Green claimed another Dornier destroyed during an early morning Channel patrol on 25 November, his victim, a 1./KG 3 Do 17Z-2 flown by Unteroffizier Joachim Cebulla, limping back to France and crashing at St Leonhard. Three of its four-man crew were killed. The following day Spitfire ace Flg Off J J 'Orange' O'Meara scored his first victory with the flight when he destroyed a Heinkel He 59 reconnaissance seaplane of *Seenotflugkommando* 3 in some style. He recalled years later:

'The presence of a "HE60" and its fighter escort approaching Dungeness was given to us by the "Y" Service unit at Capel le Ferne direct by telephone link, instead of going through the usual route via the sector control at Biggin Hill. I remember being in an awful hurry and took off in the nearest aircraft available. It was a blue-painted Spitfire (Mk IIA P7498) originally used for the early high-flying patrols, and it had specially fitted bulges in the cockpit canopy to give better pilot visibility. However, I arrived in the area plotted by "Y" and found the Heinkel without much difficulty. I never really thought about the possibility of a fighter escort, and went in from the beam. I watched it fall into the sea, then raced back. I seem to recollect I had been in the air for only 14 minutes. When I stepped out of the aircraft a rigger told me that sector had just sent through a message to intercept!'

O'Meara's He 59 had been searching for IV./JG 51's Feldwebel Adolf Rosen, whose Bf 109E had been downed by No 66 Sqn Spitfires earlier that afternoon.

Regrettably, No 421 Flt did not always have the upper hand, as Plt Off Lawrence found out to his cost early the following morning whilst undertaking the now routine solo morning patrol along the Channel coast. At 0825 hrs he encountered three Bf 109Es of 8./JG 26 undertaking a *freie Jagd* (free hunt) off Deal. He later recounted:

'Foolishly perhaps, I turned to chase them, but suddenly there was a tremendous bang, and my aircraft (Spitfire IIA P7499) simply fell apart around me. I found myself hanging in my parachute harness, dimly realising that I had been badly wounded.'

Lawrence had indeed been seriously knocked about when his Spitfire disintegrated, fracturing his right leg, lacerating his right foot and dislocating his right shoulder. Fortunately, he was rescued by a fishing trawler, and subsequently admitted to Ramsgate General Hospital. Plt Off Lawrence would not return to his unit until well into the following year.

The New Zealander had fallen victim to Oberleutnant Gustav 'Mickey' Sprick, *Staffelkapitän* of 8./JG 26, P7499 being the 22nd aircraft he had shot down since 10 May 1940. A recent recipient of the Knight's Cross, Sprick had increased his tally to 31 by the time he was killed in a flying accident when his Bf 109F-2 shed a wing due to structural failure in combat on 28 June 1941 (see *Osprey Aircraft of the Aces 11 - Bf 109D/E Aces 1939-41* and *Aircraft of the Aces 29 - Bf 109F/G/K Aces on the Western Front* for further details).

Keen to avenge the loss of Lawrence, No 421 Flt was given ample opportunity just hours later. Sgt McKay and Flg Off Baker were ordered to patrol an area of the Channel that had just witnessed a large dogfight between a mixed formation of *Jabo* and *freie Jagd* Bf 109Es from *Stab* JG 26 and I./JG 51, and Spitfires from Nos 41, 66 and 74 Sqns. Arriving on the scene 20 minutes after the initial engagement, the pair encountered a small formation of *Emils* from 2./JG 51 and proceeded to shoot two of them down five miles off Folkestone.

On the morning of 29 November the flight had a recently-arrived Spitfire IIA badly damaged in a freak accident at Hawkinge when an 18-year-old rigger by the name of 'Texas' Amer attempted to take-off in the fighter. Crashing at speed into the airfield's boundary fence, the uninjured aircraftsman was swiftly extricated and arrested. When quizzed about his actions, he replied that he desperately wanted to be a pilot! Amer was court-martialled and imprisoned for six months.

1 December saw the flight enjoy more success when a two-aircraft shipping reconnaissance patrol spotted a pair of Bf 109s 2000 ft above them up-sun near Dymchurch, on the Kent coast. Instead of attacking the *Emils*, Flg Offs Peter Hartas and Dennis Parrott inexplicably dived away, and the former was attacked by a third Messerschmitt flown by Leutnant Heidrich of III./JG 53 – Hartas later described his own tactics in his Combat Report as 'Stupid – asking for trouble'. Despite his fighter (Spitfire IIA P7498) being hit, Hartas succeeded in breaking sharply, and then managed to latch onto the second of the two *Emils* that had 'bounced' him. This Bf 109E-4 was flown by Oberfeldwebel Bernhard Seufert of 6./JG 53, and the Spitfire pilot chased it almost all the way back across the Channel before it finally crashed into the sea, killing the pilot.

On the morning of 3 December Flg Off O'Meara intercepted a solitary Do 17Z whilst patrolling on his own off Dungeness, and he claimed to have hit the bomber prior to losing it in cloud – a battle-damaged Do 17Z-2 of 5./KG 2 was later destroyed when it crashed near Estaires whilst attempting to make it back to Arras.

Forty-eight hours later 'Orange' O'Meara was in the thick of the action again as No 421 Flt enjoyed its most successful patrol to date. Led by Flt Lt Green, O'Meara and Sgt Lee surprised two Bf 109Es of II./LG 2 that were busy attacking a minesweeper off Dover. In the dogfight that ensued, 'Paddy' Green damaged one of the *Emils* (which later crash-landed with serious battle damage at Calais-Marck – Green claimed it as a probable) and 'Orange' O'Meara destroyed another. Ten minutes later the patrolling Spitfires spotted six more fighter-bombers from II./LG 2, and

O'Meara succeeded in damaging a third Bf 109E. His Combat Report, compiled by the flight's Intelligence Officer, Plt Off McLean, was later submitted to HQ Fighter Command:

'I was patrolling as second aircraft in a section of three Hurdle (No 421 Flt's radio callsign) aircraft.

'After patrolling over Deal and Dover at 10,000 ft, the Section Leader observed anti-aircraft fire over some minesweepers ten miles off Dover. On arriving at the bursts, I followed the leader in an attack on two enemy aircraft flying south below us at about 8000 ft.

'I carried out a head-on attack on the leader, who broke away to the right. After a short dogfight, I was able to get in a deflection shot from slightly astern, opening at 150 yards and closing in to about 20 yards. I broke up and away and to starboard, and I saw the enemy aircraft diving almost vertically downwards. I followed it slowly, but it flew straight into the sea about 10 or 12 miles west of Calais. After rejoining formation, we broke up south of Dungeness on being attacked by an Me 109.

'I saw the third aircraft of the section being chased by an Me 109 which was firing cannon shells at him. When the enemy aircraft broke away, I was in a position for a quarter attack, and used the remainder of my ammunition on it. The enemy aircraft emitted a thick plume of black smoke and flew westerly in a shallow dive from 5000 ft. I returned to base.'

Flg Off O'Meara's victim is believed to have been Oberleutnant Heinz Vogeler, *Staffelkapitän* of 4./LG2, who was posted missing after he failed to return to Calais-Marck in his Bf 109E-4.

As the winter closed in, Fighter Command's new Commander-in-Chief, Air Marshal Sir William Sholto Douglas, began to look forward to 1941, and consider his options. His major concern was that he would have to re-fight the Battle of Britain in the spring – something that his command was ill-equipped to do at that time. It was therefore more essential than ever that aircraft and pilots were not lost flying pointless sorties, and it seemed as if No 421 Flt might at last be used in their intended role – that of spotting enemy aircraft and reporting on their movements.

The new Air Officer Commanding (AOC) No 11 Group within Fighter Command was the ambitious Air Vice-Marshal Sir Trafford Leigh-Mallory, and one of his early orders (issued on 2 December) was that no single patrols would be flown unless absolutely necessary. As a consequence of this order, No 421 Flt began flying 'Jim Crows' over the Channel in pairs, and these flights soon began to pay dividends.

On 7 December future aces Flt Lt Billy Drake and Flt Sgt Ken Gillies (who had been wounded in action in a No 421 Flt Hurricane on 17 October) were conducting a morning patrol when they encountered a solitary Do 17 just five miles from the French coast. Despite repeatedly attacking the bomber, it failed to crash, and both pilots had to satisfy themselves with a shared probable. On the way home, Gillies' aircraft (P7498, alias the 'blue Spitfire') ran out of fuel, and he was forced to carry out a dead-stick landing at Capel le Ferne, about a mile south-east of Hawkinge.

The following day a second lone Dornier bomber was intercepted by Flg Offs O'Meara and Hartas, and although neither pilot lodged even a damaged claim following the encounter, a Do 17Z-2 from 4./KG 3 was badly damaged when it crashed near Thielt. The cause of this crash remains unrecorded, although the crew had been on a combat mission.

Yorkshireman Donald Alistair Steward McKay was one of the most successful pilots to serve with No 421 Flt/No 91 Sqn during the first months of its existence. A member of the RAF Volunteer Reserve (RAFVR), he had trained pre-war with Hurricane-equipped Nos 43 and 111 Sqns.

Called up on 6 September 1939, McKay was posted as a sergeant pilot to No 501 Sqn, again flying Hurricanes. He accompanied the unit to France in May 1940, where he destroyed three He 111s (and possibly several more aircraft that are not officially listed) prior to being evacuated back to England. McKay claimed a further three victories (all Ju 87s) during the Battle of Britain, but was wounded when shot down on 18 August by 9./JG 26 ace Oberleutnant Gerhard Schöpfel – he was one of six No 501 Sqn pilots downed on this day, four of whom fell to Schöpfel in as many minutes.

Upon recovering from his wounds, McKay was posted to newly-formed No 421 Flt, and he claimed a further nine kills and four damaged up to June 1941, when he was posted to No 55 Operational Training Unit (OTU) as an instructor. Awarded the DFM in early January 1941, McKay was commissioned in October of that year. He commenced a second tour, with No 234 Sqn, in January 1942 and quickly claimed two Bf 109Fs destroyed, before being posted as a flight commander to No 130 Sqn the following month. McKay was subsequently sent out to the Middle East, where he flew Hurricane IIs with Nos 213, 33 and 274 Sqns. Flying primarily ground-attack missions in this theatre, McKay added a solitary damaged claim (whilst flying a No 274 Sqn Hurricane IIC on 3 November 1942) to his tally of 15 kills during his time in the Middle East.

Following brief spells with a Communications Flight and the Aboukir Maintenance Unit, McKay spent the rest of his RAF career instructing, firstly in Rhodesia and then in Britain. Leaving the service in 1947, he continued to instruct within the RAFVR until June 1953. A keen aviation historian, he contributed as an author to several publications post-war until taking his own life on 30 September 1959 following the death of his wife (*via R Humphreys*)

That No 421 Flt believed the 'unless absolutely necessary' phrase in the AOC's order was obviously open to interpretation is proven by engagements involving two of the flight's most successful pilots. On the afternoon of 11 December 'Orange' O'Meara sortied on a lone reconnaissance mission to the French coast, flying at just 200 ft between Calais and Berck-sur-Mer. Using heavy cloud as cover, he spotted an enemy formation ahead of him comprised of a solitary He 59 and three escorting Bf 109Es. Undaunted by the odds, O'Meara made one swift firing pass and scattered the aircraft, before diving back into the clouds at high-speed! No claim was subsequently submitted by the pilot.

The second solo incident occurred at 1500 hrs on 17 December, and involved the equally fearless Sgt Don McKay. Sat at readiness at Hawkinge when a signal came through that a 'Dornier' was strafing Dungeness, McKay was airborne within two minutes, headed south to intercept the bomber on its way home. His Combat Report tells the story of the encounter that followed:

'I was ordered off the ground to intercept a Dornier which was machine-gunning Dungeness, and proceeded to a point about five miles south of Dungeness. I then came up through the clouds to about 4000 ft and saw what I thought was an enemy bomber dodging in and out of cloud south of me. I circled to the west to get into a strategic position in the sun and then dived onto it. I identified it as a Ju88 – not a Dornier as I had been informed – and did a stern attack.

'I used four bursts of about 300 rounds each, opening at about 250 and closing to about 100 yards. The Ju88 seemed to stand on its tail and then went down sideways, and I saw it fall into the water with a terrific splash. I did not notice any return fire.'

Although the Luftwaffe lists no losses for Junkers bombers on this day, five days earlier reconnaissance unit 4(F)./121 had a Ju 88A-5 badly shot up by no less than four No 421 Flt pilots in two separate engagements. At 0935 hrs Flg Off Hartas and Sgt Dudley Forrest claimed to have damaged a Ju 88 they encountered near Folkestone, although the bomber escaped into cloud. One hour later, Sgts Maurice Lee and Frederick Perkins engaged the same Ju 88 north-east of Sheerness, chasing it southwards into cloud. The bomber later crash-landed with battle damage near Caen.

As these actions show, a number of pilots within the flight had begun to pair up for patrols, having found that they worked well together in combat. One such duo was Peter Hartas and Dudley Forrest, who had evolved a system of signals to help them attack enemy aircraft more effectively.

Using their techniques to good effect, on 18 December they encountered a 'Dornier' (actually a reconnaissance-configured Bf 110C-2 of 3(F)./11) flying on a westerly course some ten miles east of Dover. Hartas cut off the aircraft's escape route whilst Sgt Forrest attacked it. The former then took over the attack, firing seven bursts into the stern of the aircraft. He then made successful attacks on both engines, which were left belching black smoke, before finishing off with a burst into the stern from 50 yards. The pilots reported that the 'Dornier' pulled vertically up before spiralling into the sea – the badly-damaged Bf 110 actually crash-landed near Calais.

Two other pilots who had built up an understanding in the air were Billy Drake and 'Jim' Gillies, and 24 hours after Hartas and Forrest claimed their 'Dornier', the pair also intercepted a Do 17 off Dover. As they closed in for the attack, the bomber fired its recognition lights at them, obviously mistaking the Spitfires for Bf 109s. Drake and Gillies then attacked the Dornier as it fled back towards Cap Gris Nez, and the bomber was last seen diving vertically into the undercast below. A claim of one Do 17 probably destroyed was granted by Fighter Command, the Luftwaffe admitting that at least four Dornier bombers (all from II./KG 2) were damaged on this day.

The flight had enjoyed a very successful December to date, and there was understandably much jubilation on the 20th when Flt Lt Drake was awarded the Distinguished Flying Cross (DFC) and Sgt McKay the Distinguished Flying Medal (DFM). Although these were the first decorations awarded to pilots serving with No 421 Flt, the citations for both medals also made a note of the recipients' previous wartime service with Nos 1 and 501 Sqns respectively.

Christmas Day 1940 passed quietly, with three patrols being flown despite the festivities, and it was not until the 27th that the flight encountered the enemy once again. Celebrating his receipt of the DFC, Flt Lt Drake combined with 'Paddy' Green in an attack on a 'Do 215' (actually a Do 17Z of 1./KG 3) over the Goodwin Sands. This aircraft had been engaged minutes earlier by two Spitfires from No 611 Sqn, and despite being shot up by four fighters – resulting in the death of a single crewman – the Dornier still managed to recover back to France. Drake and Green subsequently shared a probably destroyed claim.

No 421 Flt had been in existence for just over two months, and in that short time its pilots had gelled into a cohesive and effective fighting unit. Although it had been formed for a specific role, the flight found itself being used instead as a day fighter unit as the Battle of Britain drew to a close. Its pilots had achieved excellent results in these early days, before reverting to the planned role of reporting enemy aircraft movements.

Following all of these successes, the year ended on a sad note for No 421 Flt with the death of one of its original founder members, Sgt Maurice Lee. He had taken off at first light on the 31st to perform a routine weather flight, and finding that the visibility over East Kent was becoming progressively worse, had attempted to land at Biggin Hill in atrocious conditions. Striking the ground short of the airfield, Lee was killed when his Spitfire was engulfed by flames.

Having joined No 421 Flt from No 72 Sqn, Sgt Lee had made his mark with the new unit by destroying two enemy aircraft (including the flight's first claim on 15 October). He had also proven to be one of its best poor weather pilots. Indeed, on 22 December Lee had been sent aloft in thick mist to find two Wellingtons that had become lost over the Channel. One crashed, but he succeeded in guiding the second aircraft down, before having to force-land himself due to a lack of fuel. During his time with the flight Lee had experienced no fewer than four successful forced landings, including two in one day (12 December). His luck ran out on his fifth attempt.

1941 opened with a heavy fall of snow, and the first combat did not take place until 7 January when 'Orange' O'Meara and Billy Drake damaged a Ju 88 that they had found 'snooping around' between Dover and Cap Gris Nez. Minutes later Flt Lt Drake damaged a second Ju 88 in the same area.

With new leadership and a lull in enemy air activity, Fighter Command was able to go on the offensive for the first time in the war. It was decided to mount 'Circuses' using the Bristol Blenheims from No 2 Group – heavily escorted by fighter aircraft – to bomb targets in northern France, with the sole aim of 'baiting' enemy fighters into combat. Circus No 1 was flown on 10 January, the target being Foret de Guines airfield in the Pas de Calais. Although No 421 Flt was not directly involved in the operation, Flt Lt Drake and Flt Sgt Gillies did fly a post-mission 'Jim Crow' to report on the results of the Circus. Despite the raid being a small-scale affair, it was deemed a success, and offered a 'blueprint' for similar operations in the years to come. Pilots within No 11 Group were also elated to be on the offensive at last, having performed the defensive role for so long.

The following day more history was made when, after weeks of rumours, No 421 Flt was officially expanded to squadron strength and re-numbered No 91 'Nigeria' Sqn.

Apart from the title, there was little difference between No 421 Flt and the new No 91 Sqn. The role of the unit remained exactly the same, for it continued to fly special reconnaissance patrols, dubbed 'Jim Crows'. The first operation undertaken by No 91 Sqn was flown on 12 January when Flt Lt Green, Sgt Perkin and Sgt Goodwin escorted a Blenheim engaged on a 'special duty' mission over St Omer.

On the 16th Sqn Ldr F C Hopcroft was posted in from Southend-based No 611 Sqn to command the squadron, although it is unclear whether he ever actually arrived for he returned to his former unit just 48 hours later! This left Flt Lt 'Paddy' Green in command once again, being promoted to Acting Squadron Leader. He quickly organised the unit into flights, with Flt Lt Drake heading 'A' Flight and newly-arrived Flt Lt Roland Lee-Knight commanding 'B' Flight. A pre-war pilot who had entered the RAF in 1936, Lee-Knight had served with No 23 Sqn from January 1937 through to December 1940, having flown Blenheim IF nightfighters with the unit throughout the Battle of Britain. He then served briefly with Hurricane-equipped No 145 Sqn, before arriving at No 91 Sqn.

Green was delighted to be informed at this time that the unit's establishment of Spitfire IIAs had been increased to 18 aircraft to reflect its squadron status. The only problem was that the Ferry Pool had crashed five out of the eight new aircraft due for delivery!

Sgt Jackie Mann poses nonchalantly alongside the heavily damaged nose section of his Spitfire IIA (P7693) at Cheriton recreation ground following his crash-landing on 12 March 1941. The pole visible in the background of this photograph was part of the anti-invasion defences designed to prevent gliders from landing on the field. Mann had just survived being attacked by a *Schwarm* of Bf 109Fs from *Stab* JG 51 during a patrol along the Channel coast, his Spitfire being struck by several cannon rounds possibly fired from the *Friedrich* flown by then-ranking Luftwaffe ace, Major Werner Mölders. Repaired over the course of several months by Air Service Training, P7693 was issued to No 19 Sqn on 24 July 1941 and subsequently lost in action (to the pilot of a Bf 109F from I./JG 26) on the morning of 12 August during Circus 77. Its pilot on this occasion, Plt Off J L Calvert, did not enjoy the same good fortune as Jackie Mann, for he was killed in the engagement *(via M Llewellyn)*

No 91 Sqn had to wait until 22 January for its first claim, when Flg Off Parrott destroyed a Ju 88 from III./KG 1. The kill was confirmed by naval observers aboard HMS *Wasp*, who watched it plunge into the Channel between Dover and Folkestone.

By this time the Luftwaffe had largely switched to the night bombing offensive, and so with no bombers to escort, the day fighters were deployed on hunting sorties over southern England. These *freie Jagd* missions usually consisted of 'hit and run' raids on coastal towns and strafing attacks on RAF airfields. Hawkinge, being the closest airfield to occupied France, not unnaturally came in for more than its fair share of these fast, low-level and unannounced attacks.

At 1250 hrs on 4 February a Bf 109E bombed 'B' Flight's dispersal, destroying Spitfire IIA P7735 (with an incendiary cannon shell) and damaging another aircraft. The *Emil* was heavily engaged by the station's anti-aircraft guns, but according to those who watched it, the fighter 'was cleverly flown and did not appear to have been damaged'. The burned-out aircraft was usually flown by Don McKay and, in order to avenge his loss, he took off in the CO's Spitfire (P7307) and promptly destroyed a Bf 109 and damaged another off Deal (both from II./JG 3)! Upon returning to Hawkinge, he relayed the events to the squadron Intelligence Officer:

'I was patrolling between Whitstable and Dover with Sgt Gavan, just below cloud, when I spotted two aircraft below in front of me. I started to do a stall turn on them, but in doing so entered cloud and lost them. On emerging from the cloud again, east of Deal, I saw two Me109s dive out of the cloud in front of me, travelling in the same direction, and about 100 yards ahead. I immediately opened fire on the starboard one, which exploded after about five seconds. The second one climbed up into cloud, and I followed it through a gap, engaging it at about 5000 ft. I fired three bursts of about three seconds each. The enemy aircraft emitted white smoke, but I was unable to continue the attack as I had exhausted all my ammunition. I landed at Hawkinge.'

The raids continued at 1308 hrs on 8 February when Lt Werner Schlather of II./LG2 strafed Hawkinge in his red-nosed Bf 109E-7. Once again it was 'B' Flight's dispersal that was the focus of the enemy's attention, and Spitfire IIA P7615 was damaged in the *Emil's* first pass. Eyewitnesses later recounted how the German pilot literally 'stunted' over the airfield, seemingly mocking Hawkinge's AA defences. However, this was to prove his downfall, for as Schlather stall-turned over Hawkinge village in preparation for an attack on 'A' Flight's dispersal, the port wing of his aircraft was shredded by a Bofors shell. The undercarriage of the stricken fighter then dropped down as its hydraulics failed, and the Bf 109E buried itself 12 ft into the ground in a field near Arpinge Farm. Werner Schlather's body was later recovered and buried in Hawkinge cemetery.

Don McKay found himself at the centre of the action once again on 9 February whilst conducting a special weather 'recce' over the Pas de Calais area. Descending through 10/10ths cloud, he discovered that he was directly over Dunkirk Mardyck airfield. Diving down to 250 ft, he shot up the administration buildings before being chased of by a hail of anti-aircraft fire. Fortunately, both he and his aircraft escaped unscathed.

Despite the weather often being more dangerous than the enemy at this time of year, No 91 Sqn continued to carry out near-daily reconnaissance

Right
This rare air-to-air photograph shows Sgt John Down aloft in 'Paddy' Green's P7531 (featured on page seven) in early 1941. Note that by this stage in the fighter's career at Hawkinge it had swapped No 421 Flt's 'L-Z' codes for No 91 Sqn's 'DL', and that a 'Sky' fighter band had been added forward of the tailplane. The aircraft's propeller spinner had also been repainted in 'Sky', this change – along with the fighter band – being brought about by an official Air Ministry edict issued on 27 November 1940 (*via Phil Jarrett*)

sorties over the Channel. And it was whilst conducting just such a mission on 10 February that the unit suffered its first fatality. Flg Off Peter Hartas, at the controls of Spitfire IIA P7888, attempted to land at a cloud-obscured Hawkinge with the aid of 'Goose-neck' flares. However, he failed to clear a line of hills two miles south-east of the airfield and struck the ground. One of No 421 Flt's original pilots (Hartas had previously served with Nos 616 and 603 Sqns), he died before he could be admitted to hospital. The young flying officer had been married for just five days.

On 11 February Flt Lt Billy Drake was deemed to be tour-expired, and was posted to No 53 Operational Training Unit (OTU) for a rest – a veteran of the Battles of France and Britain with Nos 1 and 213 Sqns respectively, he had commanded 'A' Flight since October 1940. Drake went on to enjoy more success in North Africa, increasing his tally to 20 kills.

He was replaced as OC 'A' Flight by Flt Lt R H 'Bob' Holland DFC, who had seen much action with No 92 Sqn between May and November 1940. Wounded in combat at the height of the Battle of Britain, he had been awarded his DFC in November. Holland joined the unit from Manston-based No 92 Sqn with four and one shared kills to his credit.

On 17 February Flg Offs O'Meara and P P C 'Paddy' Barthropp (newly-arrived from No 610 Sqn, and having served during the Battle of Britain with No 603 Sqn) were on patrol when they were 'jumped' by

Below
Spitfire IIA P8194 *GOLD COAST I* was the subject of a series of official Air Ministry photographs taken at a sunny Hawkinge on 23 April 1941. Issued new to No 91 Sqn exactly two weeks earlier, it became the chosen mount of veteran ace Sgt Don McKay DFM – he flew a succession of 'M'-coded fighters throughout the war. P8194 served with the 'Nigeria' Squadron for just 24 days in total, being issued to No 234 Sqn on 3 May following the former unit's re-equipment with the Spitfire VB. Further frontline use was to follow with Nos 66 and 152 Sqns, in that order, before it was retired to No 57 OTU in early August 1942. Loaned to de Havilland in April 1943, P8194 was used on propeller landing brake trials – conducted by the company at Boscombe Down – until it was written off in an accident on 28 January 1944 *(Author's collection)*

Swung around for the benefit of the camera, P8194 reveals its right side whilst still parked in the 'A' Flight dispersal area. The presentation titling *GOLD COAST I* is clearly visible between the exhaust stubs and the cockpit. Note the bomb-damaged hangars in the distance, which were later pulled down (*via Roy Humphreys*)

three Bf 109s over Dover. O'Meara's Spitfire was badly damaged in the attack, its ailerons and radiator being holed and the cockpit quickly filling with oil fumes. 'Orange' somehow managed to limp back in the direction of Hawkinge, eventually crash-landing at Drellingore, just four miles short of the airfield. Fortunately, he was uninjured in the action, and a subsequent crash, and was therefore able to receive a well-earned DFC from His Majesty King George VI at Buckingham Palace the very next day!

No 91 Sqn would eventually become one of the more 'cosmopolitan' units in the RAF, and the tradition began on 20 February when South African Plt Off J J 'Chris' Le Roux and American Plt Off A G 'Art' Donahue were posted in. Both men had seen previous action, Le Roux being wounded flying Hurricanes in France in May 1940 with No 85 Sqn, and Donahue serving with No 64 Sqn both during and after the Battle of Britain – he too had spent time in hospital recovering from wounds suffered in combat.

They were quickly shown what august company they were in when, on 5 March, Flg Off O'Meara was awarded a Bar to his DFC, having destroyed at least 11 enemy aircraft. Then, on the 8th, Sgt McKay was also awarded a Bar to his DFM, his tally then standing at 12 aircraft destroyed. The most recent of these had been claimed just 48 hours earlier, when he engaged a Do 17Z of III./KG 3 some 15 miles south of Folkestone.

Hawkinge was bombed again on 10 March, with only slight damage being caused to the Officers' Mess, and the raid was repeated by Bf 109Es on the afternoon of the 12th. However, the score was evened somewhat when Flg Off Fisher destroyed one Bf 109 and damaged another off Dungeness. Later that day, Flt Lt Holland and Sgt Jackie Mann were patrolling the same area when they were attacked by Bf 109Fs from *Stab* JG 51. The latter's Spitfire IIA (P7693) was hit by several cannon rounds (possibly fired by then-ranking Luftwaffe ace, Major Werner Mölders), and it went into an uncontrollable dive. Despite this, and having suffered a minor wound, Sgt Mann calmly warned his flight commander of the attack, before crash-landing at Cheriton, near Folkestone.

Like his flight commander, Jackie Mann was an ex-No 92 Sqn pilot, although the bulk of his combat experience had been gained during the

Battle of Britain with No 64 Sqn – he had downed four Bf 109Es with this unit between July and September, but he had also been shot down six times, and wounded once. Despite Mann's latest brush with death, the squadron diarist recorded that 'his enthusiasm for combat remains a fine example of the spirit among squadron pilots'.

At dawn on 13 March, No 91 Sqn's early morning patrol, flown by Flt Lt Holland and Sgt Arthur Spears, succeeded in foiling an attack on Hawkinge. Five Bf 109s from II./JG 54 were intercepted, and in the subsequent chase across the airfield both pilots were credited with having shot down a fighter apiece. 'Bob' Holland's victory gave him ace status, whilst Sgt Spears (who was a nephew of World War 1 ace Maj J T B McCudden VC) had claimed his first success, and the squadron celebrated the occasion in some style.

Flt Lt Holland registered No 91 Sqn's next claim too, engaging a Bf 109 at 1500 hrs on 24 March near Hastings. He was credited with a probable, and Luftwaffe records note that a battle-damaged Bf 109F-2 from II./JG 53 force-landed at St Inglevert soon after this action had taken place.

Six days later Don McKay added another score to his ever growing tally when No 91 Sqn Spitfires patrolling off Dunkirk at 1810 hrs ran into a handful of Bf 109Es from 10./JG 51. In the brief action which ensued, the ten-kill ace succeeded in hitting an *Emil* with a series of rounds, and unbeknown to him, the fighter was written off minutes later in a crash-landing near Etaples. Thinking he had simply 'winged' his opponent, McKay only submitted a damaged claim.

On 31 March, having recovered from the minor wound sustained on the 10th, Sgt Mann was on a solo patrol over the Channel when he was attacked by four Bf 109F-1s from 7./JG 51. Throwing his Spitfire into a headlong dive from 24,000 ft in order to escape his foes, Mann lost his cockpit hood, helmet and flying goggles whilst hurtling seaward. Checking his mirror, he spied the quartet of fighters diving after him, and as he eased out of his high-speed descent at low-level, he was astonished to see a grey-dappled Messerschmitt (flown by Leutnant von Saalfeld) rocket past him straight into the Channel. Mann recovered at Hawkinge and claimed

Spitfire VB W3135 was briefly flown by No 91 Sqn stalwart Wt Off John Down following its arrival at Hawkinge in November 1941. He was posted to No 52 OTU as an instructor within days of this aircraft being assigned to No 91 Sqn, however. Boasting unusually spaced codes, W3135 was sent to the 'Nigeria' Squadron after being held in storage for six months with No 8 MU – it had been flown straight to the maintenance unit from Vickers-Supermarine. In April 1942 the fighter was sent to Air Service Training Ltd at Hamble for conversion into an LF VB, and it was subsequently modified into a low-level fighter-recce PR XIII. Issued to No 541 Sqn, W3135 was finally Struck off Charge on 26 February 1945 (*via M Llewelyn*)

a Bf 109 destroyed, his victory being confirmed by naval observers who had witnessed the action – this took Mann's overall tally to exactly five Bf 109s destroyed. Sadly, his good fortune did not last for long.

On the afternoon of 4 April elements of No 91 Sqn were scrambled to intercept Ju 88s that had been spotted harassing shipping in the Channel. The first to intercept an enemy bomber was Plt Off Douglas Gage, who damaged a Ju 88A-5 of I./KG 76 off Deal – it later force-landed at Amiens. Taking off 15 minutes after Gage, Sgts Mann (in P7565) and Spears (in P7783) headed south in search of more intruders. However, within minutes of departing Hawkinge, and whilst still slowly climbing with full tanks through 5000 ft, they were 'bounced' by Oberstleutnant Adolf Galland and his wingman Oberfeldwebel Robert Menge.

Flying on a 'private excursion over the British Isles' (as later described by Galland himself), the *Geschwaderkommodore* of JG 26 made short work of Spears' Spitfire, its pilot being struck in the right arm by an exploding cannon shell and having his legs peppered with machine gun bullets – he was Galland's 59th victim. Spears bailed out, and after landing near Dover, he was admitted to Deal's Royal Victoria Hospital.

Menge's fire had also had a telling effect on Sgt Mann's fighter as well, although the latter pilot discovered that his Spitfire was partially controllable, and he attempted to reach Hawkinge. He almost succeeded, belly-landing the stricken machine just two miles north-west of the airfield. As he scrambled clear of the burning wreck, its petrol tanks exploded and Mann sustained severe burns to his hands and face. Neither Arthur Spears or Jackie Mann would return to frontline flying.

No 91 Sqn was on the receiving end yet again on 8 April when Canadian Flg Off John Hart and Sgt Arthur Gavan were 'bounced' by elements of II./JG 51 over Manston. As with Spears and Mann, the pair were caught whilst climbing out on a patrol, Gavan belly-landing his badly damaged Spitfire (claimed destroyed by Leutnant Hans Kolbow) and Hart recovering his cannon-holed fighter at Hawkinge.

Three days later the unit at last managed to turn the tables when seven patrolling Spitfires engaged Bf 109s over the Dover Straits just after noon. Don McKay claimed yet another victory, while Flt Sgt 'Jim' Gillies, who had become separated from his squadronmates, spotted a disabled He 115 seaplane being towed by a tender towards Boulogne. Determined to attack both targets properly, he called up the new cannon-armed Spitfire VBs of No 92 Sqn from Manston and guided them to the target, which was promptly destroyed. He also helped damage

Domestic bliss at 'A' Flight's dispersal on Gibraltar Lane at Hawkinge! Sgt Don McKay cleans out a blocked drain whilst fellow sergeant pilot John Down poses for the camera and the Telephone Orderly supervises! Both pilots are on readiness alert, as they have donned their 'Mae Wests' in anticipation of a scramble *(J K Down)*

Six of No 91 Sqn's pilots – four of whom became aces – pose at Hawkinge in early March 1941. They are, from left to right, Flg Off J J O'Meara (11 and 2 shared destroyed, 1 unconfirmed destroyed, 4 probables and 11 and 1 shared damaged), Sgt J E Cooper, 'B' Flight OC Flt Lt R A Lee-Knight (5 and 1 shared destroyed, 3 probables, 3 damaged and 1 destroyed on the ground), Plt Off P P C Barthropp (2 and 2 shared destroyed, 1 probable and 3 damaged), Sgt Goodwin and Flg Off J J Le Roux (18 destroyed, 2 probables and 8 damaged). Of these pilots, only James 'Olly' Cooper failed to complete his tour with No 91 Sqn, being killed when his Spitfire VB inexplicably dived into the sea off Dungeness whilst escorting an ASR Walrus on 9 September 1941 *(Wg Cdr P P C Barthropp)*

the ship and shot down a Bf 109F (possibly an F-1 from 4./JG 53). Gillies was awarded a DFM for his part in this action on 15 May.

OPERATION *CHANNEL STOP*

In the early months of 1941 Fighter Command, in conjunction with the Royal Navy, launched Operation *Channel Stop*. Its purpose was to deny enemy shipping the use of any of the Channel ports, or to have any real freedom of movement in the Channel itself. Fighter Command's role in *Channel Stop* was to base two Hurricane squadrons at Manston specifically to operate at low-level in this area. They would be supported by a 'Jim Crow' squadron, which would patrol the enemy coast at regular intervals, seeking out enemy shipping for destruction.

Naturally enough, No 91 Sqn was chosen for the latter role, and it began patrolling on a more pre-planned basis. Two aircraft would leave Hawkinge almost on the hour, every hour, and fly across the Channel to Cap Gris Nez, before splitting up and patrolling the enemy coast alone. One Spitfire would fly up as far as Flushing, in the Netherlands, whilst the other would head down to Fecamp, in France. These were the maximum ranges for the patrols, with the usual limits being Ostend and Dieppe.

With radio silence being crucial to the intelligence gathering process, No 91 Sqn's shipping recces were always lonely affairs. The constant threat of interception by enemy aircraft meant that pilots often fought desperate battles against overwhelming odds without being able to call for help. The only option open to them was to fight their way out of trouble. Counting shipping in heavily-defended ports was always a dangerous operation, and involved some very low flying indeed. And although No 91 Sqn's role called for its pilots to simply locate and report the presence of enemy vessels, certain individuals began to exploit the opportunities available to them by attacking shipping and port installations.

The *Channel Stop* operations saw the emergence of a different breed of fighter pilot – the determined individualist who could work effectively on his own. Such pilots would become something of a trademark of No 91 Sqn over the next two years, making the unit very effective indeed in its allotted role.

Well-worn Spitifre VB W31??/'DL-W' sits in a blast pen at Hawkinge in the late summer of 1941. The exact identity of this fighter remains a mystery, although it was reportedly assigned to No 91 Sqn's OC, Sqn Ldr James Watts Farmer, at the time this photograph was taken. The weathering of the paint down to bare metal on the wing root was typical for all Spitfires that remained in the frontline for any period of time in World War 2. This was caused by the boots worn by the riggers and fitters assigned to the aircraft, who helped the pilot both strap in and unstrap, and kept the fighter in good working order when it was on the ground (*Author's Collection*)

With No 91 Sqn being very much in the frontline of Fighter Command's most active group, new pilots joining the unit had a great deal to learn in a very short space of time, and there was no substitute for operational experience. Pilot casualties and aircraft losses were an inevitable part of this process, and on 20 April Sgt E E Sykes, flying Spitfire IIA P7351, was shot down off Sandgate. Not one to waste time, he swam ashore – quite a feat considering the distance involved, the weather and the clothing he was wearing, not to mention the fact that he was slightly wounded!

Four days later Plt Off Peall also bailed out over the Channel after he lost control of his Spitfire (P7531) off Ostend following an attack by I./JG 2's Unteroffizier Amhausend. He was saved the effort of swimming home by the Margate lifeboat, which rescued him a short while later. It had been quite an introduction to squadron life for the young Rhodesian, who had joined the unit fresh from No 57 OTU just two days earlier.

The *Jagdwaffe* struck again in the early afternoon of 26 April, four *Jabo* 'tip and run' raiders from II./JG 52 dropping out of low cloud and hitting Lympne and Hawkinge just as Flt Lt 'Bob' Holland and Flt Sgt Andrew Darling were returning to base following a shipping recce flight. The latter pilot, flying Spitfire IIA P7615, was acting as 'weaver' (flying behind, protecting his leader) to Holland when they were 'bounced'. Darling succeeded in warning his flight commander of the attack, but was then caught by a burst of cannon fire from Oberleutnant Schumann's Bf 109E-7. His burned out aircraft was later found in Reindene Wood, near Hawkinge, with his body still strapped into the cockpit.

SPITFIRE VB VERSUS Bf 109F

From October 1940 onwards, RAF fighter pilots began encountering small numbers of Messerschmitt fighters which were flying faster and higher than those used previously by the Luftwaffe. Throughout the Battle of Britain the Spitfire had enjoyed a marginal performance advantage over the Bf 109E, but with the advent of the new Bf 109F, the Mk IIA was outclassed in terms of its maximum speed, service ceiling and armament. By early 1941 the *Friedrich* began to pose real problems for No 11 Group, with its squadrons suffering increasing numbers of casualties.

Losses became so serious that development work on a new mark of Spitfire (the Mk III) was halted whilst all efforts were concentrated on a 'temporary expedient' aircraft that was soon to become known as the Spitfire V. The new fighter was fitted with the improved Merlin 45 engine, producing an additional 290 hp. And although the airframe to which it was bolted was identical to the Spitfire I/II, the Mk V had a wing that housed either eight 0.303-in machine guns (the Mk VA), two 20 mm cannon and four 0.303-in machine guns (the Mk VB) or four 20 mm cannon only (the Mk VC). With its increased performance and firepower, the Spitfire V boasted performance figures remarkably similar to the Bf 109F, thus restoring the balance in the air war over Western Europe.

No 92 Sqn was the first squadron to convert to the new Spitfire, receiving its new aircraft in February 1941. There was much celebrating on No 91 Sqn when its pilots discovered that they were going to be the second unit to convert, and re-equipment was completed by 4 May.

Although the unit had been named the 'Nigeria' Squadron upon its formation, the association with the African colony did not really start until the arrival of the Spitfire V. Indeed, the government of Nigeria paid for at least 20 presentation aircraft, each of which bore the name 'Nigeria', followed by a specific province, just forward of the cockpit.

This is the full list of named aircraft:

No 91 'Nigeria' Sqn Presentation Aircraft

Lagos & Colony
Zaria Province
Warri Province
Ijebu Province (AB248)
Ilorin Province
Plateau Province (BL665)
Calabar Province
Kano Province (AD420)
Abeokuta Province
Oyo Province (AB216)

Katsina Province
Niger Province
Onitsha Province
Sokoto Province
Owerri Province
Ondo Province
Benin Province
Bornu Province
Bauchi Province
Cameroons Province

Yet another anonymous Spitfire VB! This aircraft is seen being turned around between sorties at Hawkinge during 1941. The panels covering the magazines for the cannon and machine guns can be seen laying on the ground beneath the port wing, the armourers feverishly replenishing the ammunition. Meanwhile, another airman is filling up the fighter's main fuselage fuel tank – situated forward of the cockpit – from a towed bowser parked in front of the Spitfire. The rigger sat on the cockpit entry door appears to be fiddling with the voltage regulator fitted immediately below the antenna mast – note the screwdriver in his hand (*via Andy Thomas*)

Flt Lt Jean Demozay's Spitfire VB (W3122) is refuelled from a tractor-towed bowser by LAC 'Titch' Mynard at 'A' Flight's dispersal beside Gibraltar Lane during the summer of 1941. This aircraft was issued to No 91 Sqn on 29 April 1941 in advance of most of the squadron's new Mk VBs. W3122 was frequently flown by French ace Demozay following his arrival at Hawkinge on 1 July, and although he failed to record which aircraft he used to claim his many kills, this fighter was undoubtedly responsible for some of the 18 claims he made between 10 July and 25 November. It left the squadron on 8 December 1941 and was converted into an LF VB by Air Service Training Ltd at its Hamble factory. Reissued to No 111 Sqn on 3 May 1942, the veteran Spitfire ended its days as an instructional airframe at No 10 School of Technical Training at Duxford in January 1943 (*via M Llewellyn*)

On 5 May, when Sqn Ldr Green and Flt Lt Lee-Knight flew over to Beachy Head to practice using the new cannon-armed fighters, they managed to find two Bf 109E-7s en route. These aircraft had been part of a *Jabo* attack mounted by II./JG 52 on Hawkinge and Lympne, and one of the *Emils* felt the full force of the Mk VB's increased firepower when Roland Lee-Knight hit it with several cannon rounds. His destroyed claim was rightly accepted, for the 4. *Staffel* machine crash-landed in France with 70 per cent damage. The 'hit and run' raiders had, however, already dropped their bombs when intercepted by the No 91 Sqn patrol, one of the new Spitfires (R7294, wearing the presentation name *Derrick*) being burned out when it was strafed at Lympne.

The arrival of the Spitfire VB brought with it a new role for No 91 Sqn. With effect from 5 May, the unit was to share the 'Jim Crow' work with Hurricane IIB-equipped No 601 Sqn, based at Manston. It would also undertake the new role of escorting the Lysander Air Sea Rescue (ASR) aircraft of No 277 Sqn's 'A' Flight, based at Hawkinge. ASR Lysanders located downed aircrew in the Channel, and dropped dinghies to them prior to their rescue by High Speed Launches (HSLs).

No 91 Sqn was also tasked with providing dawn and dusk patrols for the protection of Hawkinge and Lympne. The unit's efficiency in this mission was quickly tested when, on 11 May, Lympne was again attacked by Bf 109Fs of I./JG 51. They were engaged by the airfield's anti-aircraft guns and by 'A' Flight's dusk patrol, consisting of Flt Lt Holland and Sgt McKay. In the dogfight that followed, Holland damaged one Bf 109 and McKay claimed a Messerschmitt fighter destroyed.

The beginning of June 1941 saw 'B' Flight busy with low-level attacks on France. In addition to the *Channel Stop* anti-shipping operations, it attacked aircraft, troops and troop transport with some success. Whilst 'B' Flight engaged in these impromptu offensive sorties, the squadron as a whole was kept very busy with ASR escort work.

June also saw the unit bid farewell to its inspirational commanding officer, Sqn Ldr 'Paddy' Green, who had received a well-earned DFC in April. He was posted to HQ Fighter Command as Squadron Leader (Tactics), and his position at the head of No 91 Sqn was in turn taken by

Sqn Ldr James Watts Farmer DFC. The latter officer, who had joined the RAF in 1935, had seen action during the Battle of Britain with No 302 'Polish' Sqn, and then served as a flight commander with No 610 Sqn.

Three days after the departure of 'Paddy' Green, fellow No 421 Flt 'stalwart' Sgt Don McKay was posted to No 55 OTU for a rest, having claimed seven kills since joining the unit upon its formation. He had easily been the most successful pilot within No 421 Flt/No 91 Sqn during the first eight months of its existence.

Personnel from 'A' Flight pose in front of Spitfire VB 'DL-X', parked within a newly-dug blast pen at Hawkinge in July 1941. These pilots are, from left to right, Flg Off P P C Barthropp, Flt Lt Abrahams, Plt Off N P Warden (posted 'Missing' on 1 October 1941), Flt Lt J E F Demozay (OC 'A' Flight) and Sgts Connolly, J Perkin, J K Down and A Gavan. Most of them are wearing 1939 Pattern Flying Boots, with their distinctive green vulcanised canvas uppers. These proved to be a poor replacement for the all-leather 1936 Pattern Boots, as they were less than waterproof in the damp winter weather. Indeed, the moisture collected by the boots on the ground would freeze when the wearer was at altitude, causing him great discomfort. Note also the thin IFF (Identification Friend or Foe) aerial running from the tip of the tailplane to the mid fuselage
(via Andy Saunders)

South African Flg Off 'Chris' Le Roux was one of No 91 Sqn's highest scoring aces. Here, he poses with his Spitfire VB (complete with artwork below the cockpit) at Hawkinge during the summer of 1941 (IWM)

Despite the parties, farewells and welcomes, the war continued, and on 16 June four aircraft of 'A' Flight were escorting an ASR Lysander off Folkestone when they ran into four Bf 109s protecting an He 59 seaplane that was also engaged in ASR work. In the fight that ensued Sgt Connolly damaged one Messerschmitt, but the section leader, Plt Off Douglas Gage, flying Spitfire VB W3126, failed to return and was posted 'Missing'. The score was evened a little minutes later when No 1 Sqn's Hurricane IIBs, acting as top cover to the ASR sortie, destroyed the He 59.

1 July was also a day of mixed emotion. Sgt Frederick Thornber, flying Spitfire VB R7340 (presentation aircraft *Nab*), failed to return from a shipping recce to Le Touquet, and despite an extensive ASR search, no trace was found of him. It was a joy, however, to welcome Flt Lt Jean-Francois Demozay to the squadron.

Demozay of the Free French Air Force originally came from Nantes. A pre-war civilian pilot who had joined the *Armée de l'Air* in a non-combatant role upon the outbreak of war, he had been seconded to No 1 Sqn as an interpreter, and remained with the squadron until the fall of France. The unit had fled back to England on 18 June 1940, leaving Demozay on the ground with an abandoned Bristol Bombay transport aircraft and 15 groundcrew. Determined to continue the fight, he helped the riggers and fitters repair the aircraft and then flew it to England where, after training, he resumed his service with No 1 Sqn.

Arriving at No 91 Sqn following a brief spell with No 242 Sqn, Demozay already had five kills to his credit, and he soon settled in to his new role as flight commander. The unit's unique style of operational flying suited him perfectly, for he preferred to work alone, attacking targets of opportunity. Demozay did not have to wait too long to make further claims either, for on 10 July he was credited with one Hs 126 probably destroyed and one damaged whilst strafing an airfield at Boulogne.

As July continued, 'Jim Crows' were superseded by more ASR and *Channel Stop* flights. On one such sortie, on the 5th, a section from 'B'

No 91 Sqn's groundcrews worked tirelessly to ensure maximum serviceability of aircraft. Here, Cpl Brown and Flt Sgt Sam Honor tinker with the rear-view mirror of a Spitfire VB between sorties. The detachable crow bar, which doubled as a handle for closing the cockpit entry flap, is clearly exposed in this photograph. Flt Sgt Honor was mentioned in dispatches for his skill in patching up battle-damaged Spitfires *(via M Llewellyn)*

Flight was escorting an ASR Lysander when a pilot was spotted in a dinghy off the Goodwin Sands. He turned out to be Sgt Gorecki from No 303 'Polish' Sqn, who had been drifting since he was shot down during an escort mission 72 hours earlier. The next day the ASR escorts spotted a body floating in the Channel, which upon recovery was found to be that of Sgt Thornber, missing since 1 July. He had died of exposure.

On 31 July Flt Lt Demozay was on a shipping patrol over Dunkirk when he spotted four Bf 109Es. His Combat Report stated:

'I was ordered to carry out a weather and shipping recce from Ostend to Gris Nez, and took off from Hawkinge at 1710 hrs after being warned by control of the presence of several groups of enemy fighters over the French coast. I climbed to 17,000 ft and turned west, diving at speed when I reached Zeebrugge. When I reached Dunkirk, at about 4500 ft, I caught sight of four ME109Es about 500 ft below me. These were flying as two pairs line astern, with about 300 yards between the pairs, circling towards the south and approaching Dunkirk from the sea.

'My speed helped me overhaul the last pair, who did not seem to see me, and I fired a short burst with cannon and machine gun from about 200 yards as I came in astern of the rear enemy aircraft. This aircraft disintegrated after the starboard wing had come off, and the pieces fell in the sea. I fired a second short burst at its leader, which caught fire and crashed on the shore just west of Dunkirk. I then pursued the leading pair and, as the rearmost of these crossed the coast, I fired a longish burst from 300 yards. The enemy aircraft was hit and the hood came off and blew past my aircraft. I broke off combat and returned to base.'

Attacks on shipping were becoming a regular feature of No 91 Sqn's operations, and on 17 August the squadron organised an operation against a large tanker, and its Bf 109 escort, as it sailed through the Channel. The squadron formation, led by Flg Off Barthropp, rendezvoused with Spitfire VBs from Biggin Hill-based No 72 Sqn, and in a highly successful operation, Barthropp claimed one Bf 109 destroyed and one damaged, Flg Off Le Roux and Plt Off Donahue downed a Bf 109 apiece and Plt Off A J Andrews was credited with a Messerschmitt fighter probably destroyed. Additionally, No 72 Sqn also 'bagged' a Bf 109, along with a second fighter damaged – all without loss to either unit.

Three days later Plt Off Andrews was on patrol when he decided to test the flak defences by dropping an empty beer bottle from 20,000 ft over Ostend. His experiment nearly backfired, however, for as the bottle whistled down, all the ground defences opened up, forcing him to flee the area!

No 91 Sqn was fortunate to have some of Fighter Command's best pilots within its ranks, and they soon began to play their part in building up the reputation of the unit. In one such action, on 29 August, Flt Lt Demozay was on a patrol when he engaged 13 Bf 109Fs at 16,000 ft between Calais and Cap Gris Nez – in the fierce dogfight which ensued, he destroyed one and damaged another, and Flg Off Le Roux also claimed a fighter destroyed. The latter pilot went one better during the course of a shipping recce on 4 September, as his Combat Report describes:

'I was flying at 7500 ft above haze when I was told about three bandits, and more, around Boulogne to Berck-sur-Mer. When, after having had two rough vectors from control, I saw three '109s in a wide vic flying east. I attacked the one on the extreme right and gave him a three-second burst

and then I saw a cloud of black smoke and then he broke up and fell away. The leading one half-rolled and dived away, and the second one did a steep left hand turn. I just pulled my stick and turned inside him, and kept turning while firing. His tail broke up in bits and he went completely inverted and went vertically down. I then dived after him but lost him, and I was so excited, and my gyro was spinning in all directions, that I made away.'

It was another clear demonstration of the superiority of the Spitfire V over the Bf 109F, and 'Chris' Le Roux received personal congratulations for his efforts from AOC No 11 Group, Air Vice-Marshal Leigh-Mallory. The following day Sqn Ldr Watts Farmer was posted to HQ No 11 Group, being replaced by Sqn Ldr H D Cooke, who had briefly served as CO of Hurricane-equipped No 258 Sqn.

The ASR Lysanders were supplemented in September by Supermarine Walrus amphibious aircraft, which were far more effective in this role due to their ability to land on the water. Within days of their arrival, No 91 Sqn lost Sgt James Cooper on 9 September when his Spitfire inexplicably dived into the sea whilst escorting an ASR Walrus.

The ASR work was always dangerous due to the slow speeds of the rescue aircraft and launches involved, and on the afternoon of 1 October Plt Off Noel Warden and Sgt Gerald Baker were both killed in action whilst on a protective patrol for a HSL in the Channel.

Flying as a pair in a section of four led by Flt Lt Demozay, the No 91 Sqn pilots had escorted the launch to a point four miles north-west of Calais when they saw a second launch off Cap Gris Nez. Demozay and his wingman went to protect the second boat, whilst Warden and Baker remained over the original HSL. Within minutes of the formation splitting up,

One for the squadron album. The pilots of 'B' Flight gather in front of and, in the case of Sgt W G Mart, on a Spitfire VB at Hawkinge on 21 October 1941. They are, from left to right, Sgt Appleton, Sgt F H Silk, Sgt Cooper, Flt Sgt J Gillies DFM, Flt Lt J S Hart DFC (OC 'B' Flight), Flg Off A G Donahue (posted 'Missing' on 11 September 1942), Plt Off A J Andrews (posted 'Missing' on 2 November 1942) and Sgt J B Edwards (posted 'Missing' on 23 September 1942). Both Appleton and Donahue were Americans, whilst Hart was a Canadian (via M Llewellyn)

Sgt A C 'Bud' Younge of Cleveland, Ohio, also served with fellow Americans 'Art' Donahue and Sgt Appleton within 'B' Flight during 1941-42. Aside from the bold nose-art honouring his home town, Younge also christened his aircraft *"MY MARIAN"* – even his 1939 Pattern flying boots carried the name of his sweetheart on the vulcanised rubber uppers! (*via Phil Jarrett*)

Warden called up on the radio to say that he was being attacked by Bf 109s, and Demozay watched helplessly as a Spitfire plunged into the Channel, with a large force of Bf 109F-4s circling over the spot where it had hit the water. Upon returning to Hawkinge he was told that the 'Y' intelligence service at Capel le Ferne had intercepted a Luftwaffe message from a jubilant Messerschmitt pilot saying that he had shot down a Spitfire, and the second one was 'falling away'. 1./JG 26's *Staffelkapitän*, Oberleutnant Josef 'Pips' Priller, claimed one of the Spitfires for his 50th kill (out of a final tally of 101), whilst Leutnant Robert Unzeitig was credited with the second (his ninth of ten victories). An extensive ASR search over two days proved unsuccessful, and both pilots were posted 'Missing'.

On 7 October New Zealander Plt Off G C R Pannell returned to No 91 Sqn for his second tour, having previously served with the unit as a sergeant pilot. He demonstrated his skill as a fighter pilot 20 days later when the ASR Lysander that he was escorting east of the Goodwin Sands was attacked by Bf 109s. Whilst the Lysander's gunner valiantly fought off three fighters, Pannell managed to destroy one of their assailants.

His success continued the next day when he went on a shipping recce to Le Touquet and found two Bf 109Fs. He fired at one, and an enormous cloud of black smoke spewed forth from its fuselage, but he was unable to confirm the 'kill' and turned to attack the second aircraft instead. Just as this fighter fell steeply away to port after being mortally damaged, the pilot of the first Messerschmitt suddenly descended by parachute in front of Pannell, who had to take violent evasive action in order to avoid a collision. Once back at Hawkinge he claimed two Bf 109Fs destroyed.

Later that same day, at 1545 hrs, Wg Cdr James Rankin (Wing Leader of the Biggin Hill Wing) led a section of four aircraft from No 91 Sqn on an offensive operation over France. Flt Sgt Gillies and Sgt A C 'Bud' Younge, who participated in this operation as low-level decoys, decided to attack Berck-sur-Mer airfield after failing to encounter the enemy. Gillies succeeded in destroying a Bf 109 parked outside a hangar, whilst recently-promoted Flt Lt Le Roux, 'weaving' behind Wg Cdr Rankin's section, shot down another Messerschmitt to end a very successful day for the squadron – and give the South African ace status.

The Bf 109 destroyed by Jim Gillies was his last claim with the unit, for he was posted to No 59 OTU for a long overdue rest on 13 November. His departure severed No 91 Sqn's link with No 421 Flt, for he was the last of the unit's original nine pilots to be posted away.

On 17 November Plt Off Archibald Black, who had only arrived on the unit on 8 October, failed to return from an early-morning shipping recce to the Somme area that had been flown in poor weather. On the 22nd Sqn Ldr Cooke had the sad duty of writing to the missing pilot's mother:

'Plt Off Black took off from Manston at 0800 hrs on 17 November on a shipping reconnaissance along the coast of France. He had already done this same operational flight twice before, and knew the coastline. Nothing was heard from him apart from testing his wireless at the start of the flight until 0905 hrs, when he called up and said that he was climbing above

Looking suitably steely-eyed for the camera, six pilots from 'A' Flight pose outside the dispersal hut at Hawkinge in late 1941. They are, from left to right, Sgt 'Lofty' Crowford, Sgt 'Bunce' Brown, Sgt Appleton, Flg Off 'Chris' Le Roux, Flt Lt John Fletcher (OC 'A' Flight, who was posted 'Missing' on 8 February 1942) and Sgt Bill Mart (J K Down)

cloud. At the time his position was plotted as between one and two miles off Hardelot, which is half way between Boulogne and Le Touquet. He did not appear to be in the least bit worried at this time, and this was a perfectly natural action to take if he encountered low cloud and bad weather. From then onwards we were unable to make contact with him, or locate his position, and he failed to return to his base.

'At the time of the occurrence, and subsequently when he could still have been airborne, we know that there were no German aircraft in his vicinity. Therefore, there can be no possibility that he was shot down. His disappearance is a mystery to us, and I can only assume that he got lost owing to bad weather. He may possibly have force-landed in France or, if he came down in the sea, he was equipped with a rubber dinghy, and in view of his proximity to the coast, there is every possibility that he could make land.

'I am very sorry to lose your son, as he had only recently joined us, and had the makings of a very useful squadron officer. He always showed the greatest keenness in undertaking operational flights, and in the short time that we knew him, he was very popular with us all.

'I am very sorry that I cannot give you further details, but should I receive any more news I will inform you immediately. I can only hope that your anxiety will be relieved.

'Yours Sincerely,
'H D Cooke'

On 25 November Flt Lt Demozay continued his personal war against the Luftwaffe when he strafed Calais-Marck airfield, and in a typically bold attack, destroyed one Bf 109 and damaged two more on the ground. The sortie was repeated by Flt Lt Le Roux later the same day, and he too destroyed a Bf 109 on the ground.

The following day Jean Demozay was lucky to make it back to Hawkinge when his engine cut out over the Channel, having been damaged by return fire from two flak ships he had attacked off Cap Gris Nez. He radioed that he was bailing out, but as he rolled his Spitfire in order to exit the cockpit, its Merlin crackled back into life and he struggled on in the direction of the Dover coast. The engine ran, albeit very roughly, until Demozay was just five miles from the airfield, and then it cut out completely. Undeterred, he glided home, making a perfect landing!

Also fortunate to make it back to base was Sgt I W Downer, undertaking only his second operational flight over the Channel, on 27 November. He was investigating shipping in Boulogne harbour when he was attacked by Bf 109s, sustaining damage to his rudder and air speed indicator. Downer limped back to Hawkinge, but the aircraft was written off as a result of his 'wheels-up' landing.

December opened with the departure of 'Chris' Le Roux, who was posted to No 55 OTU for a rest – he was replaced as OC 'B' Flight by the recently-promoted Flt Lt John Fletcher, formerly of No 258 Sqn. At the end of the month Sqn Ldr Cooke followed the South African out of the unit, being replaced in turn by Battle of Britain ace Sqn Ldr R W 'Bobby' Oxspring DFC. The latter pilot arrived from No 41 Sqn, where he had been serving as a flight commander since September.

ENTER THE Fw 190

1941 had been an extremely busy year for No 91 Sqn, beginning with its formation, and including the intensive *Channel Stop* operations and the battle against the initially superior Bf 109F. The arrival of the Spitfire V had tipped the balance in favour of Fighter Command, and the unit had achieved excellent results in the air, on the ground and, increasingly, against enemy shipping. 1942 opened with Flt Lt Demozay's destruction of an Bf 109 on 2 January off Boulogne. This took his tally to 15 kills, and gave Fighter Command its first victory of the year.

Such good news did not last for long, however, for exactly a week later Flt Lt Fletcher encountered the squadron's first Focke-Wulf Fw 190. 'B' Flight's OC was flying a special recce mission between Paris and Boulogne when he saw the fighter and attempted to give chase. He soon realised after following it at full speed for some minutes that he was not gaining on the aircraft, so he returned to Hawkinge. This sighting was a very worrying development for the squadron because it meant that they would soon be fighting a far superior enemy once again.

As early as September 1941, RAF pilots had described a new radial-engined aircraft with performance levels far in excess of the Spitfire V. Initial reports were treated with a degree of disbelief, but by October cine gun footage had proven the existence of the new fighter – the Fw 190.

The Focke-Wulf design was indeed far superior to the Spitfire V in all operational fields, although the latter aircraft had a tighter turning circle. It was well armed, very fast and the pilot had an excellent field of view

These officers assembled for an impromptu group shot taken by a visiting *Kent Messenger* photographer outside their mess at Hawkinge one lunch-time during the spring of 1942. Among them is the Station Chaplain, the medical officer, the anti-aircraft liaison officer (known universally as 'Guns'), two intelligence officers, nine pilots from No 91 Sqn, a USAAF liaison officer and a solitary WAAF! (*via Roy Humphreys*)

These 'A' Flight personnel pose with yet another squadron mascot near their dispersal on Gibraltar Lane – Hawkinge always seemed to have more than its fair share of dogs throughout the war years! The pilot standing on the left of this foursome is New Zealander Geoff Pannell, who was later awarded a DFC for his exploits whilst serving with No 91 Sqn (*via Roy Humphreys*)

thanks to a sliding bubble canopy. The RAF now had a real problem on its hands, for although the Spitfire V had entered service almost at the same time as the Bf 109F, thus quickly negating the *Friedrich's* advantage in combat, its replacement, the Merlin 61-powered Spitfire IX, was not likely to be ready for some months – indeed, the first unit to receive the new aircraft (No 64 Sqn) did not appear in the frontline until June 1942. In the meantime, Fighter Command's loss rate soared, and the Luftwaffe became increasingly active in making devastating 'hit and run' attacks on southern towns, especially those along the coast.

February opened with the promotion and posting of Flt Lt Jean-Francois Demozay on the 1st. Much to his disappointment (he wanted to stay on an operational squadron), he was posted to No 11 Group as Squadron Leader (Tactics), and was replaced as OC 'A' Flight by Flt Lt Pannell.

Demozay would always be remembered on the squadron for both his brilliant flying and gallic rages! Leading Aircraftsman (LAC) Charles 'Titch' Mynard used to look after the Frenchman's Spitfire when he was OC 'A' Flight, and when new cockpit maps arrived on the squadron, he

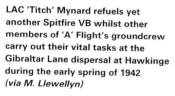

LAC 'Titch' Mynard refuels yet another Spitfire VB whilst other members of 'A' Flight's groundcrew carry out their vital tasks at the Gibraltar Lane dispersal at Hawkinge during the early spring of 1942 (*via M. Llewellyn*)

innocently placed them in the aircraft's cockpit map pocket. The engine was running when Demozay climbed in and noticed the maps. He asked, 'What is this?' to which LAC Mynard replied 'New maps, Sir'. Demozay flew into a rage, shouting 'I don't need these. I know all over France!' With that he roared off, knocking Mynard off the wing and nearly hitting him with the tailplane, before crossing Gibraltar Lane and taking off as soon as he could, raising the undercarriage when just off the ground and then executing a steep turn to starboard!

On 8 February OC 'B' Flight, Flt Lt John Fletcher, failed to return from an Ostend recce. A sergeant pilot with No 3 Sqn during the Battle of Britain, he had later served with Nos 1 and 258 Sqns prior to being posted to No 91 Sqn. Fletcher was listed as 'Missing' after an extensive ASR search failed to find any trace of him, or his Spitfire (W3132), and it seems likely that he was the squadron's first Fw 190 victim.

OPERATION *FULLER*

Since 1941 three German capital-ships, *Scharnhorst*, *Prinz Eugen* and *Gneisenau*, had been effectively trapped in the French port of Brest. Repeated attempts to bomb them throughout the year had proven unsuccessful, but by early 1942 the Germans were desperate to move the vessels to Norway, and out of harm's way. The RAF and Royal Navy intelligence services were well aware of the enemy's intentions, and Operation *Fuller* was devised in case the ships should break out from Brest.

Central to the Allied plan was 825 Naval Air Squadron (NAS), under the command of Lt Cdr Eugene Esmonde. Equipped with Swordfish torpedo aircraft, the Manston-based unit had the unenviable task of attacking the ships should they attempt to pass through the Channel.

Whilst in harbour, the vessels were kept under almost constant surveillance, although this did not stop them leaving Brest on the evening of 11 February and sailing up the Channel in broad daylight the next day.

At 1030 hrs on the 12th, Sqn Ldr Oxspring and Sgt Beaumont were on patrol when they spotted a convoy of 30+ vessels 15 miles off Le Touquet. This was the first sighting of the three ships, and it seemed incredible that they could have travelled so far without being detected. Oxspring broke radio silence to report the sighting, and upon their return to Hawkinge, Sgt Beaumont stated that he thought one of the ships was the *Scharnhorst*.

Unfortunately, further identification was not possible due to heavy flak and deteriorating weather conditions, and those in authority were reluctant to believe Sqn Ldr Oxspring's report.

The delay in taking action meant that the only attack of note was made, at 1230 hrs, when six Swordfish from 825 NAS encountered a 'wall' of flak when they attempted torpedo runs on the vessels. The entire force was shot down, with terrible losses among the crews (Lt Cdr Esmonde was later awarded a posthumous VC), and very little damage was done to the ships, which steamed into the North Sea with their E-boat escorts.

On 14 February Plt Off J P Maridor, Free French, joined No 91 Sqn from No 615 Sqn. A native of Le Havre, he had gained his civil pilot's licence at the age of 16, and when France fell he escaped to England in a fishing boat and joined the RAF. After months of trying, Maridor was overjoyed with his assignment to No 91 Sqn, for he considered that a posting to this unit offered him the best chance of attacking Germans!

The French contingent was further enlarged on the 20th when Plt Offs J Lambert and H J M de Molenes followed Maridor from No 615 Sqn. With them came veteran New Zealand pilot Flg Off 'Bob' Spurdle, who was returning to the squadron after flying catapult-launched Hurricanes with the Merchant Ship Fighter Unit since May 1941.

The squadron was fortunate to have avoided much contact with the Fw 190 up until then, but this all changed when Australian Sgt T O Omdahl was 'jumped' by III./JG 26's Oberfeldwebel Erwin Busch in a 9th *Staffel* A-1 at 1220 hrs on 24 February. Omdahl succeeded in crash-landing his fighter (W3175) at Hawkinge, but it was so badly damaged that it was duly written off – this was Busch's seventh of eight kills.

Plt Off Maridor very quickly settled into life on No 91 Sqn, becoming one of the unit's anti-shipping experts. For example, on 1 March, flying at very low level, he shot up two flak ships off Cap Gris Nez. He damaged both vessels, but his aircraft was in turn hit by flak in the port wing, and on landing at Hawkinge, the undercarriage collapsed. Maridor injured his face on the gunsight, but was otherwise unhurt. As with Flt Lt Demozay before him, the Frenchman preferred working alone, and on 12 March he flew another solo recce to Ostend, where he found a large ship and attacked it – a subsequent mission showed that it had been beached.

The squadron became involved in convoy protection work at this time, and on the same day that Maridor was strafing his ship off Ostend, Sgts

Australian pilot Sgt T O Omdahl poses with Spitfire VB *SOKOTO PROVINCE* during the early months of 1942. He was one of the first No 91 Sqn pilots to feel the full force of the Fw 190, his fighter (W3175) being jumped by III./JG 26's Oberfeldwebel Erwin Busch in a 9th *Staffel* A-1 at 1220 hrs on 24 February. Omdahl succeeded in crash-landing his fighter at Hawkinge, but it was so badly damaged that it was duly written off – this was Busch's seventh of eight kills. Note Omdahl's zippered 1940 Pattern Flying Boots, which featured a full-length front zip to allow uniform trousers or a flying suit to be tucked inside. Although more practical than previous flying boots, the 1940 Pattern was not generally favoured by fighter pilots, as it lacked the style of the 1936 Pattern issue. Pilots were also concerned about losing the 1940 Pattern boots upon bailing out of their aircraft, for the zipper made them a looser fit
(*Author's collection*)

In May 1942, the Air Ministry sent a photographer down to Hawkinge to cover the daily operations of No 91 Sqn. One of the shots that he took was this one of 'B' Flight's six Spitfire VB/Cs neatly lined up for the benefit of the camera. In the foreground is Spitfire VC AB216 *Nigeria Oyo Province*, which was flown by squadron OC, Sqn Ldr 'Bobby' Oxspring – he can be seen standing in front of his fighter. Next in line is Flt Lt F H Silk (OC 'B' Flight), with his Mk VC AA976 *GRAND HOTEL MANCHESTER*, and then Wt Off W G Mart, who was assigned a Mk VB. The remaining three pilots (all flying Spitfire VBs) have not been identified. Oxspring's AB216 enjoyed a remarkably long spell in the frontline with No 91 Sqn, being issued new to the unit on 15 March 1942, and remaining on strength until damaged on operations on 2 June 1943. Following repairs, it was used by the Aeroplane & Armament Experimental Establishment (A&AEE) in towing trials with Hotspur and Horsa gliders in conjunction with other aircraft, including a Beaufighter. AB216 was finally written on 2 February 1945 following a wheels up landing caused by an in-flight engine fire *(IWM)*

Omdahl and Crawford were protecting a convoy off Margate. During the course of the sortie, the Australian's Spitfire (AA907) suffered total engine failure, and he was forced to ditch in the sea. The aircraft quickly sank, but Omdahl was rescued by a destroyer and taken to the naval hospital at Shotley, where he was treated for minor injuries. Two days later four much-needed replacement aircraft arrived in the shape of three Spitfire VCs and one VB – they were immediately pressed into service.

March brought with it the usual coastal mist, known as the 'Hawkinge Horror', and on the 17th poor weather prevented any flying at all. The same was true at Lympne, except for a short period in the afternoon when Plt Off J R Heap and Flt Sgt Crozier were scrambled. The weather then closed in again, and they both became completely lost. Heap was vectored to Manston and landed safely, but Crozier could not be contacted because his radio was unserviceable. Attempting to land in the swirling mist, he very nearly crashed, so he climbed instead to 250 ft and bailed out. He landed safely, but his aircraft – R7338 *Papyrus* – was written off when it crashed at Park Farm, Brabourne.

In complete contrast was Flg Off Spurdle's recce to Ostend on the 25th, when he climbed to 34,000 ft in a cloudless sky and reported being able to see for miles! Four days later Plt Off Maridor flew the same recce and found several R-boats in the harbour at Nieuport. Attacking at his usual very low level, he set one alight, before beating a hasty retreat when confronted by a heavy barrage of flak. However, Maridor's controls had already been shot away, forcing him to bail out near Canterbury upon re-crossing the Channel. He landed just 100 yards from where his Spitfire, (BL261) crashed.

Maridor quickly forgot about his brush with death when he received news on 1 April that he was to be awarded a second palm to his *Croix de Guerre* for his work whilst with No 615 Sqn. Another successful pilot on the squadron was New Zealander Flt Lt Geoffrey Pannell, who made a claim on 6 April when he destroyed a Bf 109F whilst on a weather flight.

It was to be his last success for some time, however, for he was posted to Morris Motors as a test pilot just four days later.

No 91 Sqn was always fortunate in that when one good pilot left, another rapidly rose through the ranks to take his place. The unit was sad to lose Flt Lt Pannell, but pleased that the young Plt Off William Orr was fast becoming one of its anti-shipping experts. As if to prove this, on 25 April he shot up a 200-ton coaster near Nieuport, leaving it on fire and dead in the water. Two days later he was on patrol with Sgt John Edwards when they saw a large splash in the Channel. Spying a pilot in a dinghy, they guided an HSL towards the downed flyer, who turned out to be none other than Wg Cdr P H 'Dutch' Hugo, the Tangmere Wing Leader.

'A' Flight was also visited by the Air Ministry photographer, who made the six-mile journey from Hawkinge to Lympne, where the rest of No 91 Sqn was located on a semi-permanent basis. These pilots are, from left to right, Sgt I W Downer (reported 'Missing' on 29 December 1942), Plt Off H J M de Molenes (killed on 27 August 1942), Sgt R M Ingram, Plt Off J R Heap, Plt Off W B Orr (reported 'Missing' on 22 July 1942), Sqn Ldr R W Oxspring (OC, sat in the Spitfire's cockpit), Flg Off F N Gillitt, Flt Lt R L Spurdle (OC 'A' Flight), No 91 Sqn adjutant, Plt Off J B Edwards (reported 'Missing' on 23 September 1942), Flt Lt R M D Hall, and Plt Off J Lambert. The aircraft providing the backdrop is Spitfire VB *Nigeria ILORIN PROVINCE* (serial unknown), which was looked after by LAC Mynard – his girlfriend's name, Vera, is visible just forward of the cockpit entry flap *(C G Mynard)*

More 'A' Flight pilots at Lympne in early 1942. This photo was given to the Author by the late 'Spud' Spurdle, and it shows, on the ground from left to right, Sgts Hooper, 'Scotty' Downer and Ron Ingram, Flt Lt Geoff Pannell (OC 'A' Flight) and unknown. Those on the Spitfire are, from left to right, Flt Sgt Honor, Plt Off J B Edwards, unknown, unknown, Flg Off J Heap, Plt Off J Lambert, Flg Off W B Orr and Plt Off H J M de Molenes *(Sqn Ldr Spurdle)*

Keen to strike at other targets aside from ships, Plt Off Orr attacked the Dieppe gasholder on 9 May after diverting from a routine Channel recce. He left it burning fiercely.

HARD TIMES

With soaring losses among many squadrons, it was impossible to forget the Fw 190 menace, and on 10 May Sgt Downer was chased by one whilst on the near-daily Ostend recce. He was fortunate enough to be able to evade the German fighter, and returned safely to Hawkinge.

Not all of the squadron's casualties were caused by the Luftwaffe, however, with some being almost self-inflicted. On 23 May Plt Off Maridor was flying alone in the afternoon when he encountered two aircraft five miles off the French coast. He attacked one and shot it down, and only then did he recognise that it was a Spitfire VB (BM466 of No 402 'Canadian' Sqn). Maridor was then set upon by the downed fighter's wingman, barely escaping with a wounded left arm and a shot up Spitfire VC (AB170). Following a force-landing at Hawkinge, the Frenchman was admitted to Folkestone Hospital, where he met the man he had just shot down, Flt Lt D G Molloy!

There was some doubt as to who had fired first, and the argument raged for some while. However, by the time that fellow countryman Plt Off Jacques Andrieux visited Maridor in hospital, the fighting had died down, and the Canadian and Frenchman had become firm friends. Plt Off Maridor's log book was subsequently endorsed 'Failing to identify friendly aircraft before opening fire – 23rd May 1942 – reproved'.

Posed specifically for the photographer from the Air Ministry, an unnamed aircraftsman pretends to apply the finishing touches to the presentation titling on this equally anonymous Spitfire VB. The word *Nigeria* has clearly been painted on using a template (*via Phil Jarrett*)

Flt Lt Geoff Pannell sits in the cockpit of *Nigeria ONITSHA PROVINCE* (serial unknown) in one of 'A' Flight's E-Type blast pens on the western side of Gibraltar Road at Hawkinge. This photograph was taken in the autumn of 1942, following Pannell's return to No 91 Sqn for his second tour with the unit (*via Phil Jarrett*)

In a repeat of the 'B' Flight line up photograph taken at Hawkinge on a sunny day in May 1942, Lympne-based 'A' Flight was also requested to roll out all six of its Spitfires for the camera. At the head of the row is Flt Lt 'Spud' Spurdle's Spitfire VC AB248 *Nigeria IJEBU PROVINCE*, with its pilot (and his dog 'Darkie') stood proudly in front of it. Next to him is Plt Off John 'Smooth' Lambert and his Mk VB BL665 *Nigeria PLATEAU PROVINCE*, then Plt Off J 'Heapo' Heap. The remaining pilots, and their aircraft, remain unidentified (*Sqn Ldr Spurdle*)

Although No 91 Sqn was not going to be among the early squadrons to receive the latest mark of Spitfire, its pilots were initially quite pleased to take delivery of seven rare Mk VIs in late June and early July. Only 100 examples of this version of the Supermarine fighter were built, being fitted with a screw-down pressurised cabin, four-bladed propeller and extended wingtips to enable it to make high-altitude interceptions.

The aircraft was designed to counter the threat posed by Junkers Ju 86R bombers, which had appeared over Britain flying at heights of around 40,000 ft. However, following the successful interception of one of these aircraft by a stripped-down Spitfire IX on 12 September, the threat posed by the Ju 86R failed to materialise, and with most of No 91 Sqn's work being performed at low-level, the aircraft were seldom used. The Mk VI was also unpopular with pilots because it was fitted with a jettisonable hood, which was clamped down prior to take off in order to keep the

Plt Off Jean Maridor is seen some weeks after his engagement with No 402 'Canadian' Sqn's Flt Lt D G Molloy, and his wingman, on 23 May 1942. The No 91 Sqn pilot is wearing an *Armée de l'Air* tunic, with RAF wings sewn on above the left breast pocket and an unofficial Cross of Lorraine badge (the symbol of all Free French forces) pinned above the right breast pocket *(via J Holme)*

May 1942 seemed to be the month for group shots at Hawkinge, this happy band being the pilots of 'B' Flight. Their flight commander, Battle of Britain veteran Flt Lt Frank Silk, can be seen leaning on the propeller of the Spitfire. Those serving under him were typical of Fighter Command's pilots at the time, coming from all over the world. Proving this point, second from the left is American, Sgt A C 'Bud' Younge, fourth from the left is Wt Off Bill Mart from New Zealand and nearest the Spitfire on the port wing is Plt Off Jean Maridor, Free French *(Author's collection)*

cockpit pressurised. The hood could be jettisoned through the detonation of small charges built into the cockpit wall, but many pilots were sceptical that these would fire at the crucial moment, thus making bailing out an impossible task. The aircraft were soon reissued to other squadrons during the summer – two to No 124 Sqn in July, two to No 164 Sqn in September and three to Special Flight North later that same month.

By mid-summer 1942 the Fw 190 was beginning to seriously affect squadron morale. On 15 June Canadian Sgt Edwin Sykes, flying Spitfire AR370, had failed to return from a Dieppe recce, and on the 23rd 'A' Flight OC, Flt Lt 'Spud' Spurdle (by now a six-kill ace), was powerless to hunt down three Fw 190s that he spotted during a shipping recce to the Dunkirk area. The German pilots simply accelerated away from the New Zealander the moment they saw him.

On 12 July Spurdle became the hunted, rather than the hunter, when he was chased by a lone Fw 190 whilst performing a weather recce in the Somme area. Successfully evading his attacker, he then spotted four more aircraft approaching him head-on. Thinking he was about to be attacked, he fired, and then quickly recognised his 'assailants' to be Spitfires. Fortunately, Spurdle's aim was poor and no one was hit, but the encounter clearly demonstrated that even experienced fighter pilots were becoming nervous about the Fw 190.

On 11 July Sqn Ldr Demozay finally achieved his long-held ambition when he assumed command of the squadron. He had served briefly as station commander of Hawkinge, flying with No 91 Sqn whenever he could, and was delighted to command his old unit at last. Demozay's inspirational leadership qualities would prove crucial in the coming months, as his pilots struggled to come to grips with the growing Fw 190 menace.

On 15 July Flt Sgt F Y Campbell RCAF and Sgt A J Clayton RAAF were on patrol spotting off Hastings when they were 'jumped' by three Fw 190s. The Australian's aircraft (AD300) was badly hit, and with the fighter plummeting seaward in an uncontrollable spin, he took to his parachute. Once in his dinghy, Clayton was soon spotted by squadronmate Flt Lt

Canadian sergeant pilot Edwin 'Bill' Sykes had served with No 91 Sqn for over a year by the time he went 'Missing' (in Spitfire VB AR370) on a recce to Dieppe on 15 June 1942. He had cheated death soon after arriving on the unit when shot down into the sea (in Spitfire IIA P7351) some 400 yards off Sandgate on 20 April 1941. On that occasion he had fallen victim to a Bf 109, and rather than wait to be rescued, he swam ashore – quite a feat considering the distance involved, the weather and the clothing he was wearing, not to mention the fact that he was slightly wounded! On another occasion, Sykes had flown so close to the sea that three inches had been knocked off his propeller blades. His groundcrew fined him five shillings for damaging 'their' fighter! By June 1942 his luck had obviously deserted him, for he did not return from the Dieppe recce. Reflecting the fatalistic view of frontline fighter pilots in the RAF at the time, Sykes' flight commander, Flt Lt 'Spud' Spurdle, wrote in his diary:

'15th June – Sergeant Bill Sykes went missing on a recce to Dieppe. Damned shame – he was a very nice guy. Only bright thing about it was that I had his "Ray Ban" sun-glasses on "appro", and now I inherited them' (via Roy Humphreys)

Possibly the tallest pilot to serve with No 91 Sqn, Roger 'Sammy' Hall joined the unit in April 1942 and was assigned to 'A' Flight. One of the most combat-experienced pilots then in Fighter Command, he had seen action during the Battle of Britain with No 152 Sqn, flown Defiant nightfighters with No 255 Sqn (scoring the unit's first victory), and completed a tour as a flight commander with No 72 Sqn at Gravesend and Biggin Hill.

Despite his undoubted skills as a combat pilot, Hall suffered from serious bouts of depression throughout his time in Fighter Command, these usually being triggered by a chronic lack of self-confidence in his own abilities. And by the early autumn of 1942, following two years of near-constant combat, 'Sammy' Hall was a spent force emotionally, as he described in his frank autobiography, *Clouds of Fear*:

'September 17th 1942 was the day when I made my last operational flight. I had passed the point of no return. I was no longer consciously tired. I was an inanimate being actuated only by automatic reflexes. I kept very much to myself, and the death wish began to dominate my mind. I was a totally irresponsible agent, but I seemed to have acquired a sort of second wind. An unnatural abundance of energy flowed through me, and I knew that, if once I let go, I should flounder totally and never recover again, so great would be the reaction. We had only four pilots in the Flight now, and we had to be at readiness in our cockpits because the German "recce" planes and low-level fighter-bombers were coming in low over the sea, undetected by radar and inflicting damage on the coastal districts.

'Pilots in pairs spent an hour at a time at cockpit readiness and then they were relieved by the other two. We tried to read a magazine or a book or the paper at these times, though it wasn't easy. Tension was about you all the time, especially when the hands of your watch crept towards the hour when you were due to be relieved. At about five minutes to the hour the two reliefs would come out of the hut, carrying their helmets and taking the last few puffs of their cigarettes, and you wondered whether they would reach

Roger 'Sammy' Hall, who guided a rescue boat to him. There was no sign of Frederick 'Cam' Campbell (flying Spitfire BL662), however, and an ASR search failed to find any trace of him or Wg Cdr B E F 'Paddy' Finucane DSO, DFC and two bars, the Hornchurch Wing Leader (and 32-kill ace), who was missing in the same area.

More sad news followed on 22 July when popular 'B' Flight commander Flt Lt 'Billy' Orr failed to return from the Dieppe recce. Flying Spitfire BL816, he was five miles inland between Cap Gris Nez and Boulogne when he called 'Mayday', but nothing more was heard from him, and he was posted 'Missing'.

Morale was now suffering, but 'Spud' Spurdle did his best to boost it over the next few days. On the 25th he downed a Bf 109F, but his diary entry for this day reveals that he derived little satisfaction from the victory.

'Got one! An Me 109 off Calais. I needed this – he seemed green or lost or stupid. No real fun – just flew up to him and zapped him down into the sea. He bailed out too late, his 'chute not opening fully.'

Replacing tour-expired Flt Lt Frank 'Silko' Silk (who had been posted to Hawkers as a test pilot) as OC 'B' Flight in the spring of 1942, 'Billy' Orr, was posted 'Missing' from a Dieppe recce on 22 July 1942 in Spitfire VB BL816. Something of a ground-strafing specialist, Orr had developed a taste for gasholders and flak towers – and it was one of the latter that shot him down over Boulogne. 'Bob' Spurdle described his loss in the following diary entry:

'July 22nd – Billy Orr's gone. Shot down by flak over Boulogne. This was a bitter pill – Billy was a great chap, close friend and an able flight commander' (Sqn Ldr Spurdle)

Caption continued from page 42 their machines before the alarm bell sounded for take-off. If they did not, you knew damned well that you would have to go yourself.'

No 91 Sqn's Medical Officer quickly realised that 'Sammy' Hall was on the verge of a nervous brakdown, and he was immediately taken off operations and sent to an RAF hospital at Halton for psychiatric evaluation. Having suffered from mental illness soon after being commissioned in the army in 1938, Hall now realised that a second bout of clinical depression would ground him for good, and he was posted to the RAF's Administrative Branch following a long spell in hospital. Ironically, soon after being posted away from No 91 Sqn, 'Sammy' Hall was awarded a much-deserved DFC for his lengthy spell in the frontline at the height of the Fw 190 'scourge'.

This photograph of Flt Lt Hall was taken in the autumn of 1941 during his time as a flight commander with No 72 Sqn. His Spitfire VB (AA749, presentation titled Moshesh) was one of two No 72 Sqn aircraft that failed to return from a Ramrod on 8 December 1941, having been engaged by Fw 190As and Bf 109Fs of I. and II./JG 26 off Boulogne. Both RAF pilots were posted 'Missing' (via Roy Humphreys)

By contrast, his next victory, scored just 24 hours later, was anything but easy, for 'Spud' Spurdle had succeeded in downing the unit's first Fw 190, much to the delight of his squadronmates. He was on patrol off Dungeness with Flg Off E F 'Knobby' Clarkson when he spotted four aircraft above them at 8000 ft. They climbed higher to investigate, and at about 5000 ft they identified the fighters as four Fw 190s. In the five-minute dogfight that followed, Spurdle destroyed one and damaged another, whilst Clarkson (encountering enemy fighters for the first time) damaged a third. In 1986 'Bob' Spurdle described this encounter in his autobiography, *The Blue Arena*, published by William Kimber:

'Down they came – two black specks streaming thin brown trails to stain the blue behind. I throttled back, drew a bead on the leader and gave him a short burst at some 400 yards. I jinked and gave the second '190 a squirt. The guy's a clot, following his leader much too closely. He jinked violently as my guns flamed, but his leader was made of sterner stuff and never wavered as he flashed beneath me.

Undoubtedly one of Fighter Command's great characters during the early years of the war, New Zealander Bob 'Spud' Spurdle was already a six-kill ace by the time he was posted to No 91 Sqn in mid-April 1941. Following a spell with the Merchant Ship Fighter Unit, he returned to the 'Nigeria' Squadron in February 1942, and was made OC 'A' Flight in April. One of his pilots was 'Sammy' Hall, who described him in the following terms in his autobiography:

'"Spud", my Flight Commander, was small, unimposing in appearance, and almost bald. His unassuming air concealed a wealth of humour and a strong personality from those strangers to him. He had flown behind "Sailor" Malan, the top-scoring fighter pilot in the Battle of Britain, and his record and prowess in the air were impressive. Despite this, Spud had no "gongs", and it was not difficult to understand why. He had no time for senior ranks, and was unusually undiplomatic towards them. However, he did eventually get his decoration not long after I met him.'

Spurdle's typically antipodean attitude to his senior officers is revealed in his diary description of Sqn Ldr 'Moses' Demozay:

'July 15 1942 – Damn! Bob Oxspring's leaving to take over 72 Squadron from Brian Kingcome, who is being promoted to Wing Co, Kenley. This is a real blow, as Bob was a super CO and leader. It looks as if a fiery odd Frenchman who was seconded to us will take his place. "Moses" Demozay sported a "Pancho Villa" black moustache, rarely smiled and left us much to ourselves. Billy Orr, who had replaced Silko as "B" Flight Commander, and I really ran the squadron, and Moses came and went alone on his mysterious way. One day on coming in to land at Hawkinge he was obstructed by a gang-mower and, erupting in gallic rage, he fired a burst into the airfield near the tractor. The driver took off like a hare and the tractor wandered over to stall against some earthworks. We were all a little scared of Moses.'

This photo of Flg Off 'Spud' Spurdle and his dog 'Darkie' was taken at Hawkinge in March 1942 (Sqn Ldr Spurdle)

'The leader didn't seem in a hurry to turn but his No 2 was in a flap and weaved violently. Below me "Knobby" raked the second leader with a shrewd burst. I saw a cannon shell explode on the '190's shiny armoured nose and another blow a cloud of fragments from a wing.

'My Hun section was turning fast, and to avoid over shooting I chopped the throttle and went into full fine pitch. I could just get a shot at the second Hun. I followed him round, the dot fair on his cockpit, then I tightened the turn. For an instant his black spinner hung steady against "K's" nose ("K" was the code letter of Spurdle's Spitfire). I pressed the gun button and the machine guns spluttered way out on the wings while the cannons thumped and coughed. Not enough deflection.

'"K" heaved around tighter and tighter. My vision browned with partial blackout and my hands grew heavy on the stick. The '190 was somewhere below me but I held the button down for a half-second and then eased up. The second Hun whipped from under my nose and, chasing his leader, was off and away. They were going much too fast and slid up above, stall turning for another attack. I couldn't overtake them – so far I had been trying to gain height and face them head on.

'Here they come again. I pressed the gun button and the cannons' thudding drowned the machine guns' splutter. The leading Hun dipped and lifted. Suddenly, a white cloud burst down its fuselage; his tail tore off and, dragging, whipped at the end of a tangle of cables. God! I hit his oxygen bottles! Blown his bloody tail off! He flashed by, falling nose over, and my heart pounded madly. "Christ! I've blown the bastard to pieces!"

'His No 2 turned out to one side and we circled, watching the flaming wreck hurtling down. Red flames in long streamers trailed back and then a white saucer appeared – the pilot was out. Both his No 2 and I circled around the descending 'chute, then simultaneously pulled ourselves together.'

Spurdle then succeeded in damaging the second Fw 190 before his port cannon ran out of ammunition, forcing him to head back to Hawkinge. As he did so, he spotted four more Fw 190s high above him at 15,000 ft, so he dived to sea-level and returned to the airfield using low cloud as cover. His victim, Leutnant Horst Benno Kruger of 5./JG 2, was rescued by an HSL and admitted to Dover Hospital, where he was treated for a broken ankle. That evening both Spurdle and Clarkson paid the *Jagdflieger* a visit, and Kruger told them that he had destroyed 17 Spitfires, including two on 15th July – possibly Flt Sgt Campbell and Sgt Clayton.

As previously mentioned, this dogfight had been 'Knobby' Clarkson's first real engagement with enemy aircraft, and he had acquitted himself very well indeed. There was no substitute for combat experience, and it was often hard won. Indeed, a lack of it probably cost Plt Off Raymond Wildish his life on 4 August when, flying Spitfire VB BL683 on a shipping recce in poor weather, he became separated from his No 2 and did not return from the sortie. There were reports of enemy aircraft in the area at the time, and it seems likely that he was shot down.

On a happier note, Plt Off Maridor rejoined the squadron on 12 August, having been in hospital since his engagement with the Canadian Spitfires in May. He must have looked forward to being involved in Operation *Jubilee* (better known as the Dieppe raid), planned for the 19th, but he was to be disappointed. Whilst other squadrons fought desperate battles over the beaches, No 91 Sqn was given the onerous task of carrying out anti-shipping patrols between Ostend and Le Havre. With little shipping activity to report, the unit ended a poor day by scouring the Channel for downed airmen – a task it continued the following day.

Whilst engaged on these ASR searches Plt Off Edwyn Tonge, flying Spitfire VB BM558, was shot down and killed by an Fw 190 from JG 2. His loss was only slightly compensated for later in the day by Flt Lt Johnny 'Heapo' Heap's destruction of a Dornier Do 24 flying boat. The grim tale of Fw 190 victims continued on the 21st when Belgian Plt Off A Lemaire

Three of No 91 Sqn's Spitfire VBs, flown by 'Matt' Matthew, 'Andy' Andrews and Ron Batten, are seen performing a neat formation flypast over Hawkinge. This sort of flying was not the unit's strong point, as 'Spud' Spurdle explains in the following extract from *The Blue Arena*:

'Our formation flying as a squadron was a joke, but when operating as sections there was not a squadron to touch us for all-round experience' (*R M Batten*)

'A' Flight pilots take a break from standing readiness to enjoy a 'brew' from Annie's tea van at Lympne in the spring of 1942. They are, from left to right, Plt Off H J M de Molenes, Sgt R M Ingram, Sgt J B Edwards, Plt Off W B Orr, Plt Off J R Heap, Plt Off J Lambert and Sgt I W Downer. Of these men, de Molenes, Edwards, Orr and Downer were all killed in the second half of 1942 whilst serving with the 'Nigeria' Squadron (*via Roy Humphreys*)

was badly shot up by several of them five miles south of Folkestone. He managed to glide back to Hawkinge where he crash-landed, his aircraft being so badly damaged that it was later written off.

On the 25th the squadron was pleased to welcome back Flt Lt Alan Andrews and Plt Offs Perkin and Goodwin (the latter were both formerly sergeant pilots on the squadron). The following day, Andrews attempted to open a new chapter in the squadron's history by attacking a submarine. He fired a short burst at his target before realising that the submarine was, in fact, a porpoise!

The 27th saw the usual ASR searches being carried out, Flt Sgt Younge spotting a pilot in the sea without a dinghy. After a great effort, he succeeded in releasing his own, and the downed airman clung to it until he was rescued by an HSL. The rescue launches also found seriously injured Plt Off Henry 'Demo' de Molenes floating in the water off Hastings. The young Frenchman from No 91 Sqn had been engaged on the ASR search, flying Spitfire VB BL230, when his fighter ran out of fuel and he was forced to bail out. Upon departing the aircraft his head struck the tailplane and he died on board the HSL before he could be admitted to hospital.

Several days later the squadron lost three experienced officers when Flt Lts Spurdle and Heap and Flg Off Clarkson were all posted. 'Spud' and 'Heapo' were both flight commanders, and their joint posting was a serious loss – the result of somewhat harsh treatment by the Hawkinge station commander (whom Spurdle described as being 'emotionally disturbed' – this proved to be an accurate assessment, for he was invalided out of the service just weeks later and repatriated to Australia, where he shot himself on Bondi Beach). The posting arose after all three men, much the worse for wear after a long drinking session sparked by the death of the popular 'Demo' de Molenes, allowed three WAAFs to stay overnight in the

officers' mess at Reindene Wood! Flt Lt Andrews took over 'B' Flight and Flt Lt 'Art' Donahue, recently returned to the squadron from the Far East, assumed command of 'A' Flight.

Despite the fact that Plt Off Maridor had spent three months in hospital, he had not lost the art of being a fighter pilot. On 7 September he was returning from the Ostend recce when he saw a Ju 88 flying towards the Belgian coast at 1000 ft. He attacked it at 500 yards' range from astern and, despite a faulty cannon, fired 1087 rounds and observed strikes on the aircraft's fuselage and engines. Having used all of his ammunition, Maridor turned for home, but a few seconds later he saw a

In the wake of 'Bob' Spurdle's hasty departure from No 91 Sqn following the Reindene Wood WAAFs 'scandal', American Battle of Britain veteran Flt Lt 'Art' Donahue was given command of 'A' Flight at the end of August 1942. He had just returned to the squadron following a spell in the Far East fighting the Japanese, and had previously served with No 91 Sqn for much of 1941. Donahue is seen leaning on the wing of Spitfire VB *"My Marian"*, flown by fellow American Sgt A C 'Bud' Younge. The other pilots in this photograph (taken during the first week of September) are, from left to right, Flt Lt R M D 'Sam' Hall, Sgt A C 'Bud' Younge, Sgt R Ingram, Sgt F S 'Polly' Perkin, Sgt 'Johnny' Down and Sgt 'Shag' O'Shaughnessy. The squadron 'spy' (Intelligence Officer), standing alongside the roundel, is Flg Off Ely, known universally as 'The Bishop' (*via* Roy Humphreys)

Another frame from the roll of film exposed by the Air Ministry photographer at Hawkinge in early September 1942. A card school has now been started, although 'Johnny' Down seems happier tickling the throat of his pet dog and Sgt Ingram engrossed in making a point worthy of note to 'The Bishop' large orange flash on the ground as if the Ju 88 had crashed. He exposed six feet of cine gun footage during the combat, and after it had been examined, he was granted one Ju 88 probably destroyed.

On 11 September, Flt Lt Donahue (in Spitfire BL511) went on the same recce. The following Intelligence Form 'F' (Combat), submitted by the Station Intelligence Officer, details the events of this sortie:

'Flt Lt Donahue USA, No 91 Sqn, in a Spitfire left Hawkinge 0550 hrs 11/9/42 to carry out shipping recce from Flushing to Gris Nez. At 0630 hrs he was heard to send a weak three-second Mayday transmission. At the same time a message from a JU 88, operating from Schipol, was intercepted. This said that the rear gunner had been killed, one of the engines was on fire and that the enemy aircraft was attempting to get back to Brussels. It was assumed that Flt Lt Donahue had been in contact with this enemy aircraft somewhere between Flushing and Ostend. Air Sea Rescue searches were carried out for some hours by other aircraft of No 91 Sqn in this area but without success. As no other friendly aircraft was in the area of combat, it was assumed that Flt Lt Donahue had been in combat with the enemy aircraft, and had probably been hit by return fire during his attack. A claim for one probably destroyed is therefore advanced.

'Enemy casualties: 1 JU 88 probably destroyed

'Our casualties: Flt Lt Donahue USA and one Spitfire VB missing'

More posing for the camera. 'Johnny' Down points in the direction of France following a request by the photographer for his subjects to be a little more animated. Both seasoned veterans of the Channel Front, 'Art' Donahue (with field glasses – these look more like a souvenir from a night at the theatre, rather than standard military issue!) and 'Bud' Younge undoubtedly knew exactly where France was, however. Donahue was lost during a dawn solo recce of the Belgian coast on 11 September 1942 – just days after this photograph was taken. Almost certainly the victim of defensive fire from a Ju 88 that he had engaged in poor weather, the American was never found, despite an extensive ASR effort. One of those involved in the ultimately fruitless search was 'Sam' Hall, who subsequently replaced Donahue as 'A' Flight OC – a position he had filled for just six days when he was grounded for medical reasons. Already suffering from fatigue after nearly two years of frontline flying, Hall recounted post-war, 'I was not a little uncritical of Art's stupidity at the time', undoubtedly referring to his flight commander's decision to conduct the sortie in poor weather. Hall was lucky to survive the ASR flight, for thickening sea mist had reduced visibility at Hawkinge to less than 100 yards by the time he returned to base

As this official report indicates, Donahue had probably destroyed a Ju 88 during the brief action, but his aircraft had also been hit by return fire. Despite the American giving a 'Mayday' call, saying he was bailing out, the ASR search (hampered by very thick haze, which reduced visibility to 500 yards) failed to find any trace of the veteran pilot.

'Art' Donahue, who had originally joined the squadron on 20 February 1941, was briefly replaced as OC 'A' Flight by the soon to be tour-expired Flt Lt Roger Hall. He in turn was relieved of his command by Flt Lt Pannell, who returned to his beloved No 91 Sqn on 16 September.

On 23 September the dawn recce to Ostend was carried out by Plt Off John Edwards, flying Spitfire VB EN844. A radio message was received saying he was being attacked by two Fw 190s and then his radar plot faded. An ASR search failed to find any trace of him, and he was duly posted 'Missing'. He had been downed by 1./JG 26's Leutnant Artur Beese, Edwards being his sixth kill out of an eventual tally of 22.

His loss was partly avenged later in the day by the CO when an Fw 190 he was chasing stalled and crashed into the sea on its back.

Although the Spitfire V was significantly inferior to the Fw 190, it was still very effective against other enemy aircraft, and the unit continued to make claims, largely against Ju 88s, throughout the autumn of 1942. For example, on 26 September Plt Off F N Gillitt, flying Spitfire VB EN771, claimed a Junkers bomber probably destroyed, although his aircraft was hit by return fire and he force-landed at Hawkinge. Four days later Flt Lt

Sgt 'Johnny' Down is debriefed here by Flg Off Ely following a recce patrol. These missions became so routine for residents living along the Kent coast that they dubbed them 'Gert and Daisy' patrols. Down's flight mate, Roger Hall, remembers:

'The manner in which a reconnaissance was carried out was the sole concern of the pilot, and each pilot devised his own methods dependent on time of day, weather conditions, probability of enemy interception, extent of flak, and his own personal likes and dislikes. It was significant that no two pilots seemed ever to undertake a "recce" in the same way. Some flew high and others at "nought" feet. Some approached the area in question from the sea and returned along the enemy coast to base, whilst others would cover the area in the reverse direction. Some hugged the cloud base and others would brazenly ignore it and, in this way, the enemy was never certain where or when the routine "recces" would come' (via Roy Humphreys)

Andrews destroyed another Ju 88 which had passed right over Hawkinge. The Intelligence Form 'F' (Combat), submitted to HQ Fighter Command in lieu of a Combat Report, told the full story:

'Two Spitfire VBs of Black Section, left Hawkinge 1110 hours for Aerodrome Defence. After patrolling for about 20 minutes, they touched down at base owing to weather conditions, and as they did so there was considerable flak over the aerodrome. In consequence they took off again at once, even though visibility was only 800 yds and cloud almost down to ground level. Black 2 landed again almost at once at 1135 hrs. Black 1 (Flt Lt Andrews DFC), following information from controller Biggin Hill (Flt Lt Bolton), flew across the Channel towards Gris Nez at 1500 ft.

'Coming to a clear patch, he saw a Ju88 at 1000 ft, about 1000 yrds ahead of him, flying towards Boulogne in a shallow dive. The enemy aircraft at once fired off three green recognition signals and turned back in the direction of Folkestone, climbing for cloud cover. Flt Lt Andrews dived and pulled up slightly below and to starboard of enemy aircraft, now at 2000 ft. He then attacked from 150 yrds, firing a burst of six seconds from all guns. The starboard engine blew up with pieces falling off, and as Flt Lt Andrews pulled up above the enemy aircraft, the rear gunner fired a very short burst which quickly stopped. The enemy aircraft then dived steeply to port and went into cloud. Flt Lt Andrews followed, and coming below cloud saw it again.

'The enemy aircraft turned to starboard and glided towards Gris Nez, where it crash-landed on the beach with its starboard engine on fire. Flt Lt Andrews then returned to base, but took off again with Flt Lt Le Roux DFC at 1210 hrs. They saw the enemy aircraft burning furiously on the beach, and could see the column of smoke from Folkestone before landing at 1220 hrs. Flt Lt Andrews took a photograph of the burning enemy aircraft with his own camera. The Ju88 was coloured green and black with yellow in places. The black crosses were outlined in yellow, and it had the figure 5 on the fuselage.

'Ammunition: 120 rounds from cannon
      190 rounds from m/gs (2 outboard Brownings removed)

'No stoppages – cine camera exposed.

'Our Casualties: Nil

'Enemy Casualties: 1 Ju88 destroyed by Flt Lt Andrews DFC'

The removal of the two 0.303-in Browning machine guns from Flt Lt Andrew's aircraft is interesting. There was a shortage of Spitfire VCs, armed with four 20 mm cannon, and the removal of two machine guns from the VBs gave an improvement in performance against the Fw 190 which more than compensated for the loss of firepower.

On 12 October Flt Lt Andrews was on a defensive patrol with Sgt K Hawkins when they ran into four Fw 190s off Dover. The sergeant pilot (in AD548 *Delhi III*) was simultaneously attacked by three Fw 190s, and with his aircraft on fire, he dived towards the sea from 2000 ft.

The debrief given by Sgt Down following the completion of this sortie was no doubt a little more colourful than that being described to 'The Bishop' on page 49! Frustratingly, no details have emerged as to what caused this damage, when it was inflicted and where the anonymous Spitfire VB force-landed. What is known is that the aircraft was repaired and returned to service (*via Roy Humphreys*)

Struggling to get out of the burning aircraft, Sgt Hawkins stood up in the cockpit and pulled his parachute rip cord, hoping that the parachute would inflate and pull him away from the aircraft. When that failed, he turned round and started to crawl along the fuselage towards the tail of the Spitfire. Just before the blazing fighter dived into the sea, his parachute inflated and he was thrown clear and rescued from the sea within five minutes. Hawkins was taken to hospital suffering from severe shock and minor cuts and bruises. It had been a miraculous escape.

The squadron's tally of Ju 88s increased on 18 October when Flt Lt Andrews and Sgt D H Davy shot one down whilst on the Ostend recce. The bomber fired its recognition lights at them before they attacked it, leaving just the tail unit protruding from a large patch of foam in the sea.

The squadron had only destroyed one Fw 190 up to that point, but Alan Andrews and Jean Maridor came close to claiming two more on the 26th whilst on the Dieppe recce. They were warned of two enemy aircraft in the Cap Gris Nez area, and almost immediately Flt Lt Andrews was attacked from astern by a pair of Fw 190s, sustaining damage to his cockpit hood. Maridor then managed to get in behind the leading Focke-Wulf and fired a three-second burst at it from 150 yards. He saw strikes on the fuselage and wings, and the Fw 190 flicked over twice before diving away and heading inland. Flt Lt Andrews then latched onto the tail of the second aircraft, which was by now attacking Flg Off Maridor, he damaged it with a six-second burst. The two pilots returned to Hawkinge and claimed two Fw 190s damaged.

This was the damage inflicted on Spitfire VB R7292 *NEWBURY II/CAROL OR* by a well-placed 20 mm shell fired from an Fw 190A-4's Mauser MG 151/20 cannon on 26 October 1942. This shot shows the electrically-detonated shell's entry point . . .

. . . and its various exit wounds! The pattern of fragment holes that have punctured the Spitfire's thin fusleage skinning reveal that the exploding round has worked exactly as its manufacturer intended it to. This shell was designed to use its kinetic energy to penetrate its target, and then detonate to cause the maximum amount of damage. The Spitfire's pilot, OC 'B' Flight Flt Lt Alan Andrews, was lucky to escape with his life, for one of the white hot shards of metal flying around within R7292 could have easily severed the elevator or rudder cables housed inside the fuselage of his fighter. Patched up on the squadron, this aircraft remained at Hawkinge until well into March 1943 *(both photographs via G Stubbs)*

The end of October saw a change in Luftwaffe tactics, with the 'hit and run' raids on coastal towns being replaced by large-scale attacks (known as *Vergeltungsangriff*, or 'vengeance attacks') involving Fw 190s as both fighters and fighter-bombers. On the 31st Canterbury was subjected to its largest raid when 68 Fw 190 fighter-bombers, escorted by 62 Bf 109 and Fw 190 fighter aircraft, attacked the city at 1700 hrs. It was a daring raid flown at low-level, and 32 people were killed and 116 injured. A barracks and several other buildings were damaged, but the effectiveness of the city's barrage balloons had prevented further devastation.

Ten aircraft from No 91 Sqn were scrambled in response to the raid, and in fierce dogfights over the Channel, Sqn Ldr Demozay, flying Spitfire VB EP500, claimed two Fw 190s destroyed and one damaged. Flt Lt Le Roux, in Spitfire VB EN844, 'bagged' another two Fw 190s destroyed and Flg Off Maridor, flying Spitfire VB BL413, downed a single Fw 190A-4 and damaged another. It seems likely that Maridor's confirmed kill, which crashed into the sea off Cap Gris Nez, was the aircraft flown by Leutnant Paul Galland of 8./JG 26, the youngest brother of the Luftwaffe ace

Oberst Adolf Galland. Earlier in the day he had claimed a Boston of No 107 Sqn destroyed for his 17th kill in 107 combat sorties.

It had been an incredible hour's work for No 91 Sqn, resulting in its most successful day since its formation. Both the CO and Flt Lt Andrews received personal congratulations from the AOC No 11 Group for their efforts, which were marred only by the loss of Flg Off Ronald Gibbs, who failed to return from the sortie in Spitfire VB AD458. He was last seen chasing four Fw 190s, with four more on his tail.

According to JG 26's war diary, it was Gibbs who downed Paul Galland, the latter pilot having gone to the aid of 1. *Staffel's* Leutnant Artur Beese, who was being attacked by the No 91 Sqn pilot. Having despatched Galland, Gibbs was reportedly shot down seconds later by the fallen ace's wingman, Feldwebel Johann Edmann.

By November Flt Lt Alan Andrews had become one of the most successful fighter pilots then on the squadron. He had made several claims

Spitfire VB BL527 sits forlornly on its belly following a slight landing mishap at Lympne on 21 October 1942 – note that its flaps are extended and its port elevator is down and starboard elevator up! The fighter was usually flown by Plt Off Jean Maridor, and it displays his Free French Cross of Lorraine beneath the cockpit on its starboard side. BL527 never flew with No 91 Sqn again following this accident, the Spitfire being sent to Westland Aircraft Ltd for repairs to be effected, after which it was passed on to Vickers-Armstrongs for conversion into a Seafire IB *(Sqn Ldr Nash)*

One of No 91 Sqn's typically well-worn Spitfire VBs provides the backdrop for this group shot, taken at Hawkinge in October 1942. Standing in front of the fighter are, from left to right, Flt Lt Geoff Pannell (OC 'A' Flight), Sqn Ldr Demozay (OC No 91 Sqn), Flg Off Frank Gillitt, Plt Off Matthew, Flt Sgt Prytherch, Flg Off Ron Batten, Flt Lt Alan Andrews (OC 'B' Flight), Sgt Staples and Sgt Davy. Four of these pilots wear ribbons denoting their receipt of the DFC. Note also that Sgts Staples and Davy have donned their flying boots, ready for their 'Gert and Daisy' dusk patrol *(via R Humphreys)*

against enemy aircraft, and had also been successful in the anti-shipping and ground attack roles. A popular flight commander, Andrews got on just as well with his groundcrews as he did with his fellow pilots.

His wife was expecting a baby at this time, and the prospective parents had agreed on Carol as a girl's name, but could not think of a name for a boy. Reflecting the dilemma, LAC George Stubbs, who looked after Flt Lt Andrews' aircraft (R7292 *Newbury I*), painted *CAROL OR* – just forward of the cockpit!

On 2 November Alan Andrews and Jean Maridor set out on a shipping recce and ASR search to cover the French coast from Boulogne to Dieppe.

Group shots of pilots were relatively commonplace during World War 2, but photographs showing groundcrews were not. In a rare example of the latter, Sqn Ldr Demozay (far left) poses with the hard-working riggers and fitters of 'B' Flight in October 1942. These men usually served longer frontline tours than pilots, and they always considered the aircraft that they maintained to be their own property – pilots only 'borrowed' them when missions needed to be flown! Therefore, woe betide the pilot who inadvertently left his flaps in the 'locked-down' position after landing, or failed to activate his gun camera button before engaging the enemy or, worst of all, did not return the gun safety catch to the 'off' position at the completion of his sortie (*via Roy Humphreys*)

LAC George Stubbs works on Flt Lt Andrews' Spitfire VB R7292 *NEWBURY II/CAROL OR* within one of 'B' Flight's E-Type blast pens during the autumn of 1942. The artwork painted onto the fighter by Stubbs is visible just forward of the windscreen (*via M Llewellyn*)

George Stubbs pretends that he is the pilot of 'his' Spitfire, R7292. This photograph shows the exact detail of his artwork, which features both a Welsh dragon (Flt Lt Andrews came from Usk, in Monmouthshire) and a reference to the name of his pilot's soon to be born child *(G Stubbs)*

Yet another in a long line of fearsome Frenchmen to serve with No 91 Sqn, Plt Off Jean Maridor strikes a suitably stern pose in his Spitfire VB at Hawkinge in 1942 *(R M Batten)*

They left Hawkinge at 1640 hrs and headed out across the Channel. The flight was uneventful until Flg Off Maridor spotted five Fw 190s just off Le Touquet. A dogfight ensued, and the Frenchman claimed to have probably destroyed an Fw 190, which fled towards Hardelot on fire and rapidly losing height.

Flg Off Maridor then tried to find his flight commander, but despite orbiting the area for ten minutes, saw no sign of him – or of any enemy aircraft, large numbers of which were reportedly in the area. Jean Maridor returned to Hawkinge to have his worst fears confirmed. Flt Lt Alan Andrews, flying Spitfire VB AB378, had not returned from the sortie. Five Spitfires from 'B' Flight took off immediately in very poor weather to search for him, but were recalled due to worsening conditions at Hawkinge. No trace of him was found, and it was later confirmed that he had shot down by Feldwebel Adolf 'Addi' Glunz of 4./JG 26. The latter pilot was one of the most successful aces on the Channel Front, finishing the war with 71 kills (all scored in the West). Alan Andrews was his 23rd victim.

On 9 November the unit was visited by Air Marshal Leigh-Mallory, AOC No 11 Group, who presented the squadron crest, signed by the King. It featured two interlaced triangles, referring to the Governor of Nigeria's flag, over a fountain representing the sea. The motto was 'We Seek Alone' – particularly apt given the unit's principal employment!

With no improvements of note having been made to the Spitfire V during 1942, leaving it hopelessly outclassed by the Fw 190, it was remarkable that No 91 Sqn's pilots had managed to shoot down or damage a number of these fighters. Skill in the air, combined with good tactics, meant that even with inferior aircraft, pilots could still defeat the Focke-Wulf.

On 10 November Flt Sgt Downer went on a special Range Direction Finding (RDF) flight over the Channel, and 20 miles south of Dungeness he spotted two Fw 190s. Attacking them, he sent one side-slipping into the Channel, before setting off after the remaining fighter as it raced back towards France. Sadly, the superior performance of the Fw 190 meant that he never got within range of his quarry, and he had to abandon the chase.

As the winter closed in, conditions at Hawkinge became increasingly difficult, with frequent prolonged periods of very thick mist and fog. The

'B' Flight pilots, and their 'Spy', wait around between sorties at Lympne in November 1942. They are, from left to right, unknown, 'Dave' Davy, Ron Batten, 'The Bishop' and Johnny Round *(Sqn Ldr Nash)*

squadron had always used Lympne in periods of bad weather, and it was decided to make the move a permanent one during the winter of 1942 – 'B' Flight moved on 15 November, followed by 'A' Flight eight days later.

Although the airfield was fairly standard in layout, the officers were billeted off-base at Port Lympne, a luxurious mansion overlooking Romney Marsh. Pre-war, the house had been owned by Sir Philip Sassoon, Under-Secretary of State for Air, and had seen many famous guests in the 1930s. However, it is unlikely that any of them enjoyed themselves as much, or appreciated the luxury to such a degree, as the pilots from Lympne!

On 6 December Flg Off Gordon Dean and Flt Sgt Melville Eldrid were flying the Dieppe recce when they were attacked by two Fw 190s from 6./JG 26 that were flying an identical mission. In the brief engagement

Flg Off Gordon Dean sits in his Spitfire VB, which he named *P.D.Q.* This proved to be a misnomer, however, for on 6 December Dean (in either BL536 or AB982) and Flt Sgt Melville Eldrid were shot down by two Fw 190s from 6./JG 26 during the routine Dieppe morning patrol. The German pilots were flying an identical mission to their RAF counterparts, and during a brief engagement Leutnant Kurt-Erich Wenzel and Unteroffizier Gerhard Vogt made short work of their opponents *(Sqn Ldr Nash)*

Gordon Dean's wingman on that fateful 6 December Dieppe patrol was Melville Eldrid, who is seen here just weeks earlier clowning around with his dog 'Rex' at Lympne *(Sqn Ldr Nash)*

More damage inflicted by 20 mm rounds fired from an Fw 190. This anonymous Spitfire VB limped back to Lympne on 11 December 1942, having been struck both in the upper fuselage and battery compartment door. The skilled riggers on No 91 Sqn would have had this damage patched up within days, just as long as the aircraft's structural framing (clearly exposed) had not been hit *(Sqn Ldr Nash)*

Officers serving with No 91 Sqn in 1942-43 enjoyed arguably the best quarters available to any frontline flying unit in Fighter Command whilst based at RAF Lympne, for they revelled in the opulent surroundings of Port Lympne, a luxurious mansion overlooking Romney Marsh. Pre-war, the house had been owned by Sir Philip Sassoon, Under-Secretary of State for Air, and had seen many famous guests in the 1930s. In this December 1942 photograph taken outside the entrance to Port Lympne, Flg Off J A Anstie, Flg Off G H Dean, Plt Off J K Down and Flg Off R S Nash prepare to take the winter air during a stroll around the mansion's extensive lawned areas *(Sqn Ldr Nash)*

that followed, Leutnant Kurt-Erich Wenzel and Unteroffizier Gerhard Vogt made short work of their opponents. Fighter controllers back in England feared the worst when both Spitfire radar plots faded just north of Dieppe. Posted as 'Missing', neither pilot was ever found. Incredibly, 24 hours later almost to the minute Plt Off J P 'Coudray' (it is believed his real name was J P Lux), Free French, was also posted 'Missing' when his Spitfire VB (BL853) was downed north-west of Calais whilst flying the Ostend recce. He had fallen victim to 1./JG 26's Feldwebel Franz Hiller.

Sqn Ldr Demozay was promoted to wing commander on the 8th and posted to Dover as the Army Liaison Officer. During his time as CO of No 91 Sqn, the unit had enjoyed great success, but he was a very private

man and preferred to work alone. The squadron had led a very active social life throughout 1942, but he seldom took part in it, spending a great deal of his off duty time by himself. His replacement was Sqn Ldr Ray Harries, who was posted in from No 131 Sqn, where he had served as a flight commander. He had already made several claims, and he relished the prospect of commanding his own squadron – with him came a new squadron dog, a German shepherd by the name of 'Wg Cdr Boris'!

1942 had been a hard, but ultimately successful, year for No 91 Sqn. The fight against the vastly superior Fw 190 had been costly in terms of pilots and aircraft lost, and yet there had been successes. Several examples of the much-vaunted fighter had been destroyed or damaged, and the squadron had also inflicted considerable damage on other enemy aircraft, as well as ships and ground targets.

Flt Sgt 'Scottie' Downer (posted 'Missing' on 29 December 1942), and his new bride, Joyce, pose outside the church for a few formal snaps just moments after 'tying the knot'. To the right of Mrs Downer is Plt Off John Edwards, who was also posted 'Missing' (from the Ostend recce) on 23 September 1942. Downer was Flt Lt Roger Hall's closest chum on No 91 Sqn, and he spoke of him with great affection in his autobiography:

'The pilot I knew best, the one I liked the most and spent the best part of my time with was "Scottie", a flight-sergeant and a New Zealander. I seemed to know him the moment I met him, as though I had encountered him in some previous existence. When we did dawn or dusk patrol with two aircraft, he used to arrange it so that we did it together and the same applied when we were engaged in air-sea rescue escort. He always came with me in my car and, as he hadn't learnt how to drive, I taught him.

'He was 22 and much the same sort of build as I was. He was always cheerful and laughed a lot. He hadn't a great deal of confidence in himself since his first trip, when he did just about the most stupid thing possible and dived through the flak barrier at Boulogne to strafe a U-boat lying in dock there. He never tired of recounting this story, and admitting how bloody stupid it had been' (Sqn Ldr Nash)

Sadly, the year ended with more losses, including Sgt Jack Chittick on 18 December. He was flying Spitfire VB EP508 on patrol with Sgt A G O'Shaughnessy when they were attacked from astern by two Typhoons from Manston-based No 609 Sqn. Sgt O'Shaughnessy managed to evade them, but Sgt Chittick lost his life when he was shot down in flames.

Eleven days later Plt Offs I W 'Scottie' Downer and W G Mart were patrolling between Dungeness and Beachy Head when they were attacked from astern by two Bf 109Gs. The one-sided engagement was described by Flt Lt Roger Hall in his autobiography *Clouds of Fear,* published by Bailey Brothers and Swinfen in 1975:

'Scottie was on the outside of the two and they were in loose line abreast. This was our customary formation when working in pairs, the idea being that both could observe the other's tail. Number two said that they were flying just beneath the cloud base, which was nearly ten-tenths. The first intimation he had that all was not well was when he saw two '109s emerge from the cloud and just sit on Scottie's tail. He said he didn't have time to warn Scottie on the R/T about them. "It all happened so quickly. It was over before I could turn towards them", he told us, overcome by emotion. "They went back into the cloud almost before Scottie had hit the water and then I came back to base".'

An ASR search by the Hawkinge Lysander failed to find any trace of 'Scotty' Downer, or his Spitfire VB (EN782). The popular New Zealander had served on the squadron since November 1941, and he had only been commissioned on 17 December.

NEW YEAR, NEW HOPE

1943 was to be a year of enormous change for No 91 Sqn, and it began with a move back to Hawkinge on 11 January. Bad weather prevented much flying, but on the 20th the cloud dissipated sufficiently enough for the Luftwaffe to launch an ambitious attack on London. A large force of fighter-bombers from JGs 2 and 26 attacked the city at 1200 hrs, with the raid taking the RAF completely by surprise. Twelve Spitfires from No 91 Sqn were scrambled, but were unable to intercept the aircraft before they had bombed South London, with devastating results.

Sqn Ldr Harries was at RAF West Malling testing a new throat microphone when he heard of the raid, and he immediately scrambled, heading for Pevensey. Intercepting four 'Bf 109Fs' (these were almost certainly G-models), Harries destroyed one and damaged a second fighter, before being attacked by four Fw 190s. Exploiting the Spitfire V's superior turning circle, he pulled back firmly on his control column and managed to get in behind the rear Fw 190, hitting it with a number of cannon rounds before hastily returning to Hawkinge.

In the meantime Flt Lt R S Easby and Plt Off B Fey had been warned of bandits at 14,000 ft off Deal. Climbing into the sun, they became separated, and Fey suddenly felt his aircraft (Spitfire VB BL333) become uncontrollable. Although he had seen no enemy aircraft, he had obviously been hit, and he bailed out from 12,000 ft. It took him 20 minutes to finally reach the sea, but he was only in the water for one-and-a-half minutes before being rescued by an HSL! Fey had fallen victim to Oberleutnant Klaus Mietusch, *Staffelkapitän* of 7./JG 26, who downed a Spitfire VB of No 332 'Norwegian' Sqn over France later in the same sortie. These

Flg Off Ron Batten was shot down by return fire from a Do 217 that he succeeded in destroying over the Channel on 9 February 1943. Unlike a number of his contemporaries posted 'Missing' at this time, he managed to force-land in France and was quickly captured. Prior to their demise, Ron Batten and his specially-modifed Spitfire VB 'P-Peter' (AD261) had proven the worth of cameras when undertaking shipping and coastal recce flights (*PRO – Air 27/742*)

two successes were kills 27 and 28 for the highly experienced Mietusch, who had increased his tally to 75 by the time he was killed in combat with USAAF P-51Ds whilst leading III./JG 26 on 17 September 1944.

From late 1942 onwards, No 91 Sqn had been using the Spitfire LF VB, which was a version of the standard VB optimised for low-level operations – the unit's 'stock in trade'. The LF VB was fitted with a Rolls-Royce Merlin 45M engine with supercharger modifications to make it more effective at low altitude, whilst its distinctive pointed wingtips were removed, reducing the span to 32 ft 6 in. These modifications enabled the LF VB to dive, accelerate and roll faster, and also gave it a five miles per hour speed improvement at 10,000 ft and below. Although many of No 91 Sqn's LF VBs had been modified and reissued following hard use as standard Spitfire VBs with other squadrons, the unit used them to good effect in many anti-shipping sorties, and against Fw 190s.

'No 91 PHOTO RECCE UNIT'

February began with very poor weather, and few sorties were flown. By the 5th, however, conditions had improved sufficiently for some shipping recces to be flown, and Flg Off Ron Batten took off in search of enemy shipping in Boulogne harbour. Ever since 1941, when the *Channel Stop* operations had begun, No 91 Sqn's pilots had complained bitterly that their aircraft were not fitted with cameras. It was difficult enough flying in heavily defended areas without having to count shipping at the same time, and the oblique cameras would have made life a lot easier for them.

Very little was done about their complaints until Spitfire AD261 (an LF VB) was fitted with an F24 oblique camera. The aircraft – coded 'P for Peter' – was usually assigned to Flg Off Batten, who developed a keen interest in aerial photography, and so flew the modified Spitfire whenever possible. His first success with the camera was on a shipping recce to Boulogne on 5 February, when he photographed a large vessel in the harbour, having already shot up a train near St Valéry-en-Caux.

Flt Lt Ian Matthew was OC 'B' Flight in early 1943, and he is seen here posing with his Spitfire VB *Nigeria ONDO PROVINCE*. As with most frontline units, the two flight commanders on No 91 Sqn effectively ran the unit on a day-to-day basis. Ex-'A' Flight OC 'Bob' Spurdle recounted in his post-war autobiography;

'I was very conscious of the power invested in me – I would decide who flew and when. I would decide if the pilot concerned was fully capable of a particular job, or when he should be sent out on his own at risk in the interest of his training and furthering of experience.

'As a flight commander I could recommend (through the CO of course) that a chap needed rest, deserved a gong, should be posted as unsuitable and so forth. But the hardest part was to stand before the board, chalk in hand, and allot the days' flying with its terrible risks to friends.

'Let's not beat about the bush – the position could be grossly abused. I knew flight commanders who enhanced the chances of ridding themselves of unwanted aircrew by giving them extra dangerous missions, or an unfair share of them.

'There and then I swore to myself that if I didn't care for a chap, or if his flying was not to my liking, and so a probable risk to others, then I'd have him posted elsehere. My pilots could trust me and I them – with our lives.'

Another former 'A' Flight OC in Roger Hall was unfazed by his responsibilities during his time with No 91 Sqn:

'Rank was a thing to which little or no significance was attached. Apart from the CO himself, there were over half a dozen flight lieutenants in the squadron, of which I was one, but their duties were in no way different from those of the other pilots. The two flight commanders, of course, had the administrative authority consistent with their position, but even this involved little beyond the duties of those in the remainder of the squadron' *(Author's collection)*

Four days later Batten and 'P for Peter' were scrambled from Hawkinge to intercept a Do 217 which was bombing Hastings. At 1055 hrs a series of radio transmissions between the pilot and Sqn Ldr Igo, the Biggin Hill fighter controller, were recorded as follows:

Flg Off Batten – 'Course for base please.'
Sqn Ldr Igo – 'Vector 340 – Any luck?'
Flg Off Batten – 'Yes, destroyed the aircraft'
Sqn Ldr Igo – 'Nice work, come back 340.'
Sqn Ldr Igo – 'Your position should be five miles west of Gris Nez.'
Flg Off Batten – 'My aircraft is u/s. I may have to bail out just over coast of France.'
Sqn Ldr Igo – 'Keep flying 340.'
Flg Off Batten – 'I shall have to bail out – have destroyed one.'
Sqn Ldr Igo – 'Keep transmitting'

Nothing further was heard from Ron Batten, who had crash-landed in France and was quickly captured.

Although 'P for Peter' had been lost, other aircraft on the squadron had by then been fitted with cameras too, and several pilots began to take

Known as 'The Bishop' to all and sundry on No 91 Sqn, Flg Off Ely served as the unit's Intelligence Officer from 1941 to 1943. It was his task to interview pilots making claims, record their stories in the form of Combat Reports and, when he was satisfied, submit them to HQ Fighter Command for official confirmation *(PRO – Air 27/742)*

excellent photographs of enemy shipping. In fact the photographic sorties pioneered by Ron Batten had become so successful that the squadron had begun to call itself 'No 91 Photo Reconnaissance Unit'!

On 10 February the unit was warned of a 5000-ton raider that was expected to pass through the Channel at any moment. The following day Flt Lt I G S Matthew (OC 'B' Flight) found the vessel in the outer harbour at Boulogne, and a constant watch was maintained both on the warship and its five escorts.

An early recce on the 12th revealed that it was still there, and so the squadron Intelligence Officer, Flg Off Ely, went to RAF Ford to brief the crews of a Boston bomber squadron, who bombed it at 0930 hrs the next day. No 91 Sqn's new 'ace' photographer, Sgt 'Shag' O'Shaughnessy, was then despatched to Boulogne to photograph the vessel at very low-level – upon returning to base, his imagery revealed that it was undamaged. At 1400 hrs that same day 20 Ventura bombers set out to attack the ship once again, but the raid was recalled due to poor weather.

Conditions failed to improve on the 14th, and the vessel left Boulogne during the night. Several recces by the squadron failed to locate it, but late on the 15th Flg Off Van de Velde found it in No 5 dock at Dunkirk, taking three excellent photos of the ship The saga continued until the 27th, when the vessel slipped away at 1100 hrs, thus evading the Venturas that were scheduled to bomb it three hours later!

On 4 March Sqn Ldr Harries and Flg Off R S Nash were on patrol over Dungeness when they were told of two bandits flying north-west from Boulogne. They climbed to 15,000 ft and spotted an Fw 190 which, on seeing them, immediately dived. Harries and Nash dived down after it, and as the descent became faster and faster, the CO observed that his indicated air speed was 460 mph! With great difficulty, the two Spitfire pilots pulled out of the dive at 2000 ft, but the Fw 190 continued down-

Plt Off Jim Johnson poses in his distinctive dark blue uniform favoured by most Australian pilots serving in the RAF during World War 2. On 8 March 1943 Johnson was posted 'Missing' when he failed to return from the Ostend recce in Spitfire AB894 (*The Hallow Spitfire*). No trace of him, or his aircraft, was ever found, and his squadronmates believed that he was yet another victim of the Fw 190 (*Sqn Ldr Nash*)

With a longer spinner, revised national markings and clipped wings, this Spitfire LF VB is typical of the aircraft that equipped No 91 Sqn during the first months of 1943 (*J T Watterson*)

ward at an ever increasing speed – visual contact was lost at about 1500 ft. Five seconds later a large explosion was seen on the ground two miles inland from Calais, exactly where the Fw 190 was diving, and the claim of one Focke-Wulf destroyed was allowed by HQ Fighter Command.

Although No 91 Sqn had made several claims against the Fw 190, it still posed a major threat to pilots, and on 8 March Plt Off Jim Johnson RAAF, flying Spitfire AB894 (*The Hallow Spitfire*), was posted 'Missing' when he failed to return from the Ostend recce. In the absence of evidence to the contrary, it seemed likely that he was yet another Fw 190 victim.

Sixteen days later, at 1000 hrs on the 24th, 15 Fw 190A-5s from 10./JG 54 attacked Ashford. Led by the legendary Oberleutnant Paul *'Bombenkeller'* Keller, the fighter-bombers hit the Kentish town hard, killing 50 and injuring a further 77 – this was the worst single loss of life suffered in the county during the entire war. Unable to prevent the surprise attack, No 91 Sqn intercepted the raiders as they headed back across the coast for France (minus their leader, who had been lost over Ashford town centre, either to flak or the explosion of his own bomb). Flg Off J A Anstie, flying Spitfire LF VB BL410, and Flg Off R G H de Hasse, in Spitfire LF VB W3425, were patrolling between Hawkinge and Dungeness when they saw four aircraft heading out to sea.

Thinking they were Spitfires, the pilots followed them and then realised to their horror that they were Fw 190s. The German fighters turned sharply and attacked Anstie and de Hasse head on. BL410 was damaged almost immediately (by Feldwebel Wilhelm Freuwörth of 5./JG 26, who claimed the Spitfire as his 57th of 58 kills – he downed a No 609 Sqn Typhoon for his final victory 24 hours later), which prevented its pilot from returning fire, and as he turned for home, he saw W3425 dive into

'Spy Mk II'. Flg Off R M Miller replaced 'The Bishop' as No 91 Sqn's Intelligence Officer in early 1943 (PRO – Air 27/742)

the sea. Belgian pilot Raymond de Hasse, who was on his very first operational sortie, was never seen again. He had fallen victim to 5./JG 26's Unteroffizier Peter Crump, who survived the war with a tally of 23 kills from 202 combat missions.

Flying for his life, Flg Off Anstie took evasive action across the Channel until Sqn Ldr Harries and Plt Off O'Shaughnessy, who had been scrambled from Hawkinge, fought off the attacking Fw 190s. Sqn Ldr Harries (in EP496) promptly destroyed one of the two Fw 190s that were attacking Anstie (no aircraft were reported as lost by the Luftwaffe), and then he and PO O'Shaughnessy shared in damaging another.

Having almost certainly had his life saved by his colleagues, Anstie tried to reach Hawkinge, with his aircraft streaming Glycol. This proved to be impossible, however, so he headed for Lympne instead and crash-landed just short of the airfield, sustaining head injuries and bruising. Anstie's aircraft was written off as a result of the damage.

On a lighter note was Flt Lt Matthew's mishap on 7 April. Coming in to land at Hawkinge after completing a mundane patrol, he found the wind blowing at between 60 and 70 mph. Just as he touched down a gust caught his aircraft and tipped it onto its nose. Uninjured, and obviously unconcerned by the accident, Matthew climbed out saying 'I always land like that – it saves the brakes'. His humour quickly evaporated, however, when he remembered that he was flying the CO's aircraft!

No 91 Sqn had been operating Spitfire VBs since May 1941, and struggling against the Fw 190 since early 1942. Shortly after the death of Flg Off de Hasse, rumours began to circulate that the unit was about to be re-equipped with the latest variant of Spitfire, the F XII. This was the first production model to be fitted with the Rolls-Royce Griffon engine, and it would quickly prove itself to be the RAF's answer to the low-flying Fw 190.

The rumours were confirmed in mid-April, when No 91 Sqn was ordered to redeploy to RAF Honiley, Warwickshire, to become the second, and last, Fighter Command unit to convert onto the Spitfire F XII.

No 91 Sqn's entire roster of pilots pose for an 'end of term' photograph with the Spitfire LF VB at Hawkinge in April 1943. They are, from left to right, Turner, Anstie, Maclean, Todd, Benson, Hoornaert, Telfer, Matthew, Ingram, Harries (CO), Kynaston, Pannell, Mart, Huntley, Down, Johnson, Easby, Naismith and Bond. Within days of this shot being taken these men had commenced their conversion onto the Spitfire F XII *(Sqn Ldr Nash)*

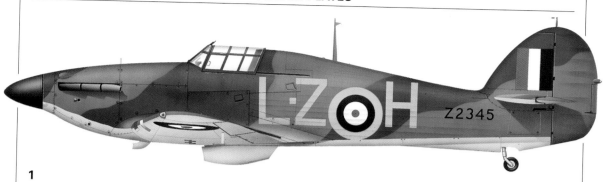

1
Hurricane IIA Z2345 of Sgt Frederick Perkin, No 421 Flt, Gravesend, October 1940

2
Hurricane IIA Z2352 of Flg Off Dennis Parrott, No 421 Flt, Gravesend, October 1940

3
Spitfire IIA P7499 of Plt Off Keith Lawrence, No 421 Flt, Hawkinge, November 1940

4
Spitfire IIA P7531 of Flt Lt Charles Green, OC No 421 Flt, Hawkinge, November 1940

5
Spitfire IIA P7307 of Sgt Donald McKay, No 91 Sqn, Hawkinge, February 1941

6
Spitfire IIA P8194 *GOLD COAST I* of Sgt Donald McKay, No 91 Sqn, Hawkinge, April 1941

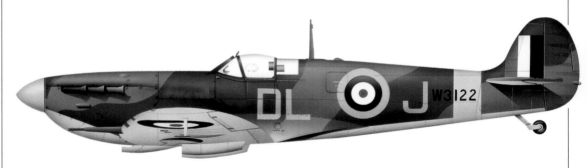

7
Spitfire VB W3122 of Flt Lt Jean Demozay, No 91 Sqn, Hawkinge, July 1941

8
Spitfire VB W3135 of Sgt John Down, No 91 Sqn, Hawkinge, November 1941

9
Spitfire VC AA976 *GRAND HOTEL MANCHESTER* of Flt Lt Frank Silk, No 91 Sqn, Hawkinge, May 1942

10
Spitfire VC AB216 *Nigeria OYO PROVINCE* of Sqn Ldr Robert Oxspring, No 91 Sqn, Hawkinge, May 1942

11
Spitfire VB AB248 *Nigeria IJUBU PROVINCE* of Flt Lt Robert Spurdle, No 91 Sqn, Lympne, May 1942

12
Spitfire VC AB170 of Plt Off Jean Maridor, No 91 Sqn, Hawkinge, May 1942

13
Spitfire VI (serial unknown) of Plt Off Jean Maridor, No 91 Sqn, Hawkinge, August 1942

14
Spitfire VB R7292 *NEWBURY II/ CAROL OR* – of Flt Lt Alan Andrews, No 91 Sqn, Hawkinge, September 1942

15
Spitfire LF VB BL527 of Plt Off Jean Maridor, No 91 Sqn, Hawkinge, October 1942

16
Spitfire LF VB BM543 of Flt Lt Geoff Pannell, No 91 Sqn, Lympne, December 1942

17
Spitfire LF VB AD261 of Flg Off Ron Batten, No 91 Sqn, Hawkinge, February 1943

18
Spitfire LF VB (serial unknown) of Sgt John Watterson, No 91 Sqn, Hawkinge, March 1943

19
Spitfire F XII EN625 of Sqn Ldr Ray Harries, OC No 91 Sqn, Hawkinge, May 1943

20
Spitfire F XII MB832 of Flg Off Jean Maridor, No 91 Sqn, Hawkinge, May 1943

21
Spitfire F XII MB830 of Flt Lt Ian Matthew, No 91 Sqn, Hawkinge, May 1943

22
Spitfire F XII MB836 of Flt Sgt Fred Lewis, No 91 Sqn, Tangmere, February 1944

23
Spitfire F XIV RM617 of Flg Off Jacques Andrieux, No 91 Sqn, West Malling, May 1944

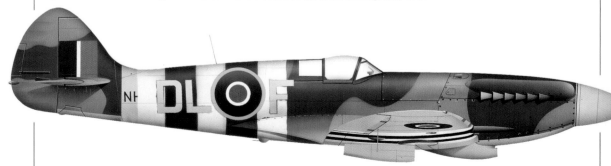

24
Spitfire F XIV NH698 of Flg Off Ken Collier, No 91 Sqn, West Malling, June 1944

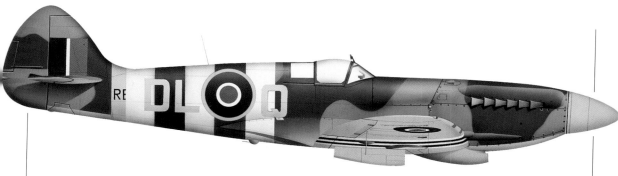

25
Spitfire F XIV RB169 of Flt Lt Ray Nash, No 91 Sqn, West Malling, July 1944

26
Spitfire F XIV RB185 of Sqn Ldr Norman Kynaston, OC No 91 Sqn, West Malling, July 1944

27
Spitfire F XIV RB188 *BRÜMHILDE* of Flt Lt 'Johnny' Johnson, No 91 Sqn, West Malling, July 1944

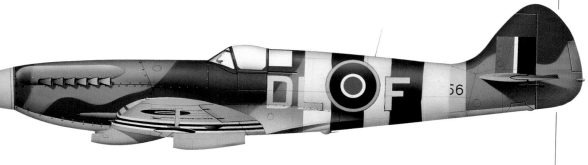

28
Spitfire F XIV RM656 of Flt. Lt. Jean Maridor, No 91 Sqn, Deanland, July 1944

29
Spitfire LF IX MK734 of Plt Off Fred Lewis, No 91 Sqn, Deanland, August 1944

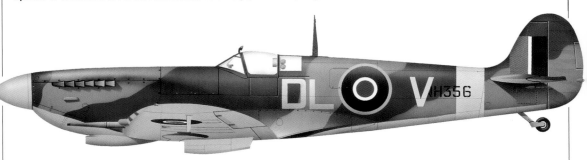

30
Spitfire LF IX NH356 of Sqn Ldr Peter Bond, OC No 91 Sqn, Manston, December 1944

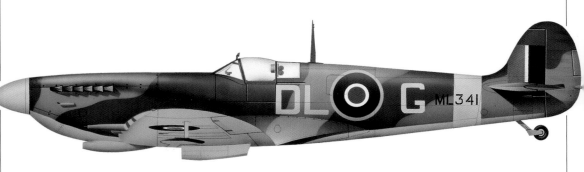

31
Spitfire LF IX ML341 of Flt Lt John Draper, No 91 Sqn, Manston, February 1945

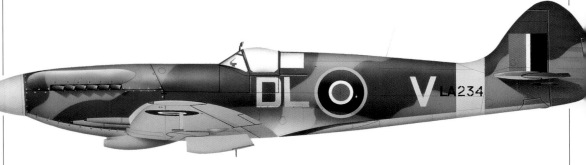

32
Spitfire F 21 LA234 of Flt Lt Roy Cruickshank, No 91 Sqn, Ludham, April 1945

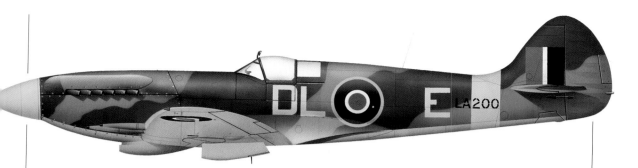

33
Spitfire F 21 LA200 of Plt Off Geoff Kay, No 91 Sqn, Ludham, May 1945

Official crest of No 91 'Nigeria' Sqn

NEW AIRCRAFT, NEW ROLE

No 91 Sqn arrived at Honiley on 20 April 1943, and conversion to the new Spitfire began the next day. The switch to the F XII went well, if a little slowly for the unit, which was desperate to return to Kent with the latest mark of Spitfire! They did not have to wait long though, returning to Hawkinge on 21 May with 12 brand new aircraft.

A few days later, at 2150 hrs on the 25th, Sqn Ldr Ray Harries and Plt Off J A Round had just landed from a low patrol of the Hastings/Rye area, and Flg Off Maridor and Plt Off Davy were waiting to land from the same patrol, when they were scrambled again to intercept 12 to 15 Fw 190s approaching Folkestone at sea level. The German fighter-bombers scattered as soon as they were attacked by the No 91 Sqn section, all except one aircraft dropping its bombs into the sea.

In the ensuing dogfight the CO destroyed two Focke-Wulfs, Maridor and Round one each and Davy probably destroyed a fifth – all without loss to the squadron. Plt Off Round described this memorable action in his Combat Report, compiled on his return to Hawkinge:

'I had just landed with Blue Leader and was taxying back to dispersal when the Flying Control fired the "scramble" signal. I took off at once and headed towards Folkestone, where I saw a lot of flak. I saw two Fw 190s flying parallel with the coast westwards on the deck, and watched them jettison their bombs. I tried to attack the leader but could not get enough deflection and did not fire. I climbed up and saw two more, heading out to sea, so followed them and selected the No 2, who was being left behind by his leader. I chased him for about ten miles until I was about 200 yards behind him, at the same time trimming my aircraft. I found myself sud-

Sqn Ldr Ray Harries' Spitfire F XII, EN625, photographed at Hawkinge just days after the unit had returned to its traditional home on 21 May 1943. Harries was flying EN625 on 25 May 1943 when he claimed No 91 Sqn's first victories with the new F XII – two Fw 190s destroyed over the Channel off Folkestone. This particular fighter had been issued to No 91 Sqn on 13 May 1943, and it remained with the unit until No 91 Sqn had fully converted to F XIVs on 9 March 1944. During its time with the 'Nigeria' Squadron, EN625 was frequently used by Flg Off Ray Nash, who was flying it on 16 June 1943 when he destroyed an Fw 190, and again on 20 October that same year when he downed a Bf 109G. Following a period in storage, the aircraft was used by No 451 'Australian' Sqn, the Fighter Leaders' School and the Air Fighting Development Unit, before it was lost in a forced-landing in Norfolk on 11 December 1944 *(Sqn Ldr Nash)*

Another view of EN625, showing the Spitfire F XII's clipped wings to good effect. These, along with the aircraft's superb Griffon engine, made the revised Supermarine fighter an effective Fw 190 *Jabo* hunter (*Sqn Ldr Nash*)

denly pulling up on him very quickly, and gave a burst of about three seconds from full astern. His nose went down and he went straight into the sea. I continued chasing the other but lost sight of him in the failing light. As I turned to go back I saw a big splash some way to the west as if an aircraft had gone in.

'I claim one Fw 190 destroyed.'

The action was witnessed by many local people in Folkestone, No 91 Sqn preventing what would have been a devastating raid on the town. Having recently suffered so much damage at the hands of 'hit and run' raiders, it was a great boost to civilian, as well as RAF, morale, and *The Folkestone Herald* proclaimed 'RAF Smash Hit and Run Raiders' on the front page of its 26 May edition. The squadron's pilots became local heroes, with the men involved in this particular action being presented with gifts, including engraved silver tankards. Such acts cemented a friendship that lasted long after the unit had left Hawkinge.

Congratulations also came from the Mayor of Folkestone, whilst C-in-C Fighter Command, Air Marshal Sir Trafford Leigh-Mallory, sent the following signal:

'To: OC No 91 Sqn (R) 11 Group
'From: HQ Fighter Command

'C.64 261800 – Heartiest congratulations on your fine achievement yesterday. Well done No 91 Sqn.

'Leigh-Mallory.'

The pilots were delighted with the Spitfire F XII, which proved to be extremely effective against the Fw 190, especially at low altitude. On 6 June Plt Off Davy and Sgt J T Watterson were on patrol south of

Illustrating the change in equipment experienced by the pilots assigned to No 91 Sqn during the early months of 1943, Sgt 'Wattie' Watterson sits 'at readiness' in Spitfire LF VB *Nigeria SOKOTO* at Hawkinge in early 1943 . . .

Hastings when they saw bombs falling in Eastbourne. They immediately altered course to intercept the raiders as they made good their escape, and soon spotted an Fw 190A-5 about three miles away, flying at sea level.

Thanks to the increased horsepower of the Griffon engine, they easily overhauled the fleeing fighter-bomber and attacked it together. Sgt Watterson finished it off with a three-second burst from 100 yards, the aircraft hitting the sea and breaking up – some of its debris caused minor damage to Watterson's aircraft. Both pilots jointly claimed one Fw 190 destroyed.

The raid on Eastbourne was carried out by 7. *Staffel* aircraft of *Schnellkampfgeschwader* (SKG) 10, the 'hit and run' experts who had been terrorising southern England since April 1943. The unit had been formed as the fourth *gruppe* of SKG 10 following the amalgamation of 10.(*Jabo*)/JG 2 and 10.(*Jabo*)/JG 54. The Eastbourne operation was typical of those flown by the *gruppe* during 1943, and was described in detail by one of the participating pilots, Leutnant Helmut Wenk, in the *Blitz - Then and Now Volume 3*, published in 1990 by Battle of Britain Prints International:

. . . and just weeks later prepares to fly a patrol in Flt Lt Ian Matthew's Spitfire F XII MB830 *(both photographs via J T Watterson)*

'As we neared the target (Eastbourne) we shifted from our cruising formation, line abreast by *Schwärme*, into our attack formation, line astern. At the same time we opened up to full power, flying about ten metres above the sea to avoid the British radar. Just before we crossed the coast the leader pulled up to about 300 metres and we followed, turning in to attack. Plunging down through the flak, we released our bombs in a *Steckruben-wurf* ('turnip lob') shallow dive attack, then got back to low level and curved round to port to escape round Beachy Head and out to sea.'

At 0609 hrs on 16 June, Yellow Section of No 91 Sqn left Hawkinge to escort a No 277 Sqn ASR Walrus which had been sent to pick up a Polish pilot in his dinghy in the Channel. The rescue was successful, but the sea state was too rough for the Walrus to take off again, so it started to taxi back to Dover.

Soon after this operation had started, the Walrus and its No 91 Sqn escorts were attacked by about 20 Fw 190s from II./JG 26. A dogfight developed, during which Flg Off Ray Nash claimed to have destroyed one Focke-Wulf and damaged another, whilst Belgian pilot Flg Off V P R Seydel, flying Spitfire EN627, destroyed a second Fw 190 before being shot down himself (no German losses were recorded on this day). He managed to bail out, but was unable to release his parachute or dinghy, having sustained a broken arm and leg, as well as head and back wounds. No 91 Sqn's Red Section arrived and, by making repeated dives, guided HSL 2547 to Seydel, who was rescued and taken to Dover Hospital.

Although the Spitfire F XII had again proved itself against the Fw 190s, which quickly broke off the combat despite the odds being in their favour, they were still dangerous adversaries, having shot down both Seydel and Sgt Willie Mitchell (in MB835), who was missing from the operation. The German pilots were credited with destroying four Spitfires, II./JG 26's *Gruppenkommandeur*, Hauptmann Wilhelm-Ferdinand *'Wutz'* Galland (Adolf Galland's middle brother), claiming one to take his tally to

Revelling in the low altitude performance of the Griffon III engine, a No 91 Sqn pilot performs a high-speed pass over Hawkinge in Spitfire F XII 'DL-E' soon after the unit had returned to Kent in May 1943 *(Sqn Ldr Nash)*

WAAFs work on a No 91 Sqn Spitfire F XII at Hawkinge during the summer of 1943. Parked behind the fighter is a Miles Master III and a Spitfire IX *(via M Llewellyn)*

'Wg Cdr Boris' served both as Sqn Ldr Harries' faithful companion and No 91 Sqn's mascot. Here, he takes one final look at Hawkinge prior to moving with the unit to Westhampnett in late June 1943 *(PRO – Air 27/742)*

42 – he had scored 55 kills by the time he met his death in action on 17 August 1943. 4./JG 26's Oberfeldwebel *'Addi'* Glunz was credited with another, for his 35th victory, whilst his *Staffelkapitän*, Oberleutnant Horst Sternberg, 'bagged' his 18th (of 22 – he was killed on 22 February 1944). The final victory should have gone to Feldwebel Peter Crump, although he did not bother submitting a claim.

Soon after this engagement had taken place No 91 Sqn was notified that it was leaving Hawkinge to form a Spitfire F XII wing with No 41 Sqn at RAF Westhampnett, in Sussex. The last 'Jim Crow' was flown on 25 June, and the unit's departure saw the biggest Hawkinge party for some years. 'Wg Cdr Boris' was not forgotten either, as he was presented with a collar inscribed 'From the CO and Officers of RAF Hawkinge'.

No 91 Sqn's time at Hawkinge had been extremely successful, with 77 enemy aircraft destroyed, 27 probably destroyed and 78 damaged. The results in the air had seen its pilots rewarded with one DSO, eleven DFCs (and four Bars) and five DFMs (and one Bar).

RAMRODS, RODEOS & RHUBARBS

The squadron moved to Westhampnett on 28 June, this airfield being the satellite station for the famous RAF Tangmere, situated at the foot of the South Downs. As soon as the squadron arrived, it commenced flying operations which would last, with few breaks, for nearly a year.

These sorties were divided into three types – Ramrod, which was a fighter-escorted bombing attack on a short-range target(s); Rodeo, which saw fighters sweep over enemy territory; and Rhubarb, where small-scale fighter and fighter-bomber formations attacked targets of opportunity.

The first wing operation was flown on the 29th, Wing Leader, Wg Cdr Rhys Thomas DSO, DFC leading the squadrons on Ramrod 114, which saw them escorting Eighth Air Force B-17s sent to bomb Le Mans. From then on the squadron was involved in one type of operation or another almost every day. The work was often tedious, with the Luftwaffe usually choosing to stay on the ground, but the pilots were forced to maintain the highest state of vigilance in case they did attack.

And on 18 July German fighters did just that. The wing was escorting Typhoons that had been sent to attack Abbeville as part of Ramrod 148 when they were engaged by a mixed force of between 25 and 50 Fw 190s and Bf 109s (several of the latter were identified as the G-models, with their underslung 20 mm cannon) from II./JG 2. In the dogfight that followed, Sqn Ldr Harries destroyed three Bf 109s whilst flying MB831, taking his tally of kills to ten and four shared.

Routine servicing is carried out on a Griffon II engine at Hawkinge in June 1943. Aside from the two groundcrew working on the fighter, Flg Offs Van de Velde, Prince de Merode and Anstie also pose for the camera *(Sqn Ldr Nash)*

These would prove to be Harries' last claims as CO of the squadron, however, for he was promoted to wing commander on 19 August and posted just down the road to take charge of the Tangmere Wing. His place as CO of No 91 Sqn was in turn taken by the 'A' Flight commander, Flt Lt Norman Kynaston.

Like his predecessor, the new CO preferred to lead from the front, and on 24 August he was at the head of No 91 Sqn as it participated in Ramrod 215. During the operation, the wing strafed Bernay and Beaumont airfields, and Yellow Section (comprising 11-kill ace Flg Off Gray Stenborg DFC, RNZAF, Flg Off Mart and Flt Sgt B G Mulcahy) was attacked from astern by Bf 109s. The trio of Spitfire pilots quickly managed to shake the Messerschmitt fighters off, and each pilot went on to claim a share in the destruction of a Bf 109.

TOP SQUADRON

September was to be an outstanding month in the history of the squadron, and began with the unexpected move of the Tangmere Wing to Lympne for anti-shipping patrols – these lasted from the 1st to the 4th inclusive.

The week did not begin well, however, for Wt Off J M Bishop, flying Spitfire EN230, was forced to ditch in the sea off Dover with engine trouble on the very first day of operations. He was rescued from the sea by the Royal Navy, suffering from shock and bruises, but otherwise uninjured. He was extremely lucky to have survived this harrowing episode, being the first pilot to have successfully ditched a F XII. Bishop had only managed to free himself from the wreckage of EN230 after it had already sunk 30 ft below the surface of the water.

The work at Lympne consisted mainly of shipping patrols and the usual bomber escort work, and on the 2nd the squadron flew Ramrod S24. As Blue Section was about to rendezvous with the bombers, Flt Lt Matthew's

Flg Off Gray Stenborg DFC, Plt Offs 'Shag' O'Shaughnessy and Bill Mart, Flg Off Ron Ingram and Flt Lt Geoff Pannell DFC and *Croix de Guerre* try each others' caps on for size! Both Stenborg and Pannell were New Zealanders *(Sqn Ldr Nash)*

Shopwyke House was No 91 Sqn's 'home' whilst the unit was based at Westhampnett and Tangmere. This photograph of the beautifully restored mansion was taken in 1992 (*Author*)

Plt Off Colin Ettles poses in a rather over-sized aircrew sweater outside Shopwyke House during the summer of 1943. His audience includes several WAAFs and 'Wg Cdr Boris' (*Sqn Ldr Nash*)

aircraft developed engine trouble and he was forced to turn for home, accompanied by his No 2, Flg Off G W Bond. At 12,000 ft over Le Touquet, the pair encountered four Bf 109Gs, and a brief skirmish developed. Matthew fired a two-second burst at one Messerschmitt, which dived into the ground near Le Touquet, but he was then attacked from astern by another aircraft. Fortunately, Flg Off Bond was looking after his flight commander, and the second Bf 109 was swiftly shot down into the sea.

The spell at Lympne ended in fine style on the 4th when the squadron flew Ramrod S31, escorting Marauders sent to bomb St Pol marshalling yards. On the return journey the close escort was attacked, and Sqn Ldr Kynaston led No 91 Sqn (in MB803) down from 12,000 ft to join in the melee. Having evaded two Fw 190s, the CO saw another attacking a Spitfire from astern, and he managed to get in behind it, firing from 200 yards. The aircraft burst into flames, turned over and dived into the sea, with the pilot bailing out – this was Kynaston's first confirmed kill. In the meantime, Gray Stenborg (flying MB805) was battling with two more Fw 190s, easily out-turning them and shooting one down into the sea from a distance of just 50 yards and then damaging the second fighter.

The squadron had suffered no casualties since joining the Tangmere Wing, highlighting again how effective the Spitfire F XII was against the Fw 190 and Bf 109G. Casualties were an inevitable part of air warfare, though, and on 8 September Flg Off Stenborg, Plt Off C R Fraser and Flt Sgt R A B Blumer RAAF were 'jumped' by four Bf 109Gs whilst flying Ramrod S41 (escorting Mitchells bombing Vitry-en-Artois airfield). Fraser's MB852 was severely damaged, and he was forced to bail out near the target. Quickly captured, he spent the rest of the war as a PoW.

The remaining three fighters succeeded in breaking off the combat and headed for home, and whilst flying back over Lille, Flt Sgt Blumer spotted two Fw 190s about 400 yards away. He attacked one and observed strikes on it, black smoke pouring from the fighter's engine and pieces flying off. Gray Stenborg then watched it dive into the ground, thus confirming 'Red' Blumer's first claim.

Blumer was in action again on the 16th, when the squadron flew Ramrod 223, escorting bombers to Beaumont-le-Roger airfield. The sortie was uneventful until the squadron arrived over the target, and the CO (again in MB803) led an attack on ten Fw 190s from 4./JG 26. In the dogfight that followed, he destroyed one Focke-Wulf (flown by Unteroffizier Franz Gasser, who was killed when his Fw 190A-5 crashed near Cormeilles), whilst Stenborg (in MB805) and Frenchman Lt Jaques Andrieux (flying MB839) each destroyed a Bf 109G. On the way home Flt Sgt Mulcahy's Spitfire (EN617) developed engine trouble, and he limped back in the company of his fellow Australian, Flt Sgt Blumer. Blumer's second Combat Report for the day told the story of what happened next:

'When covering his going out of France, six '190s attacked us. I broke into them, broke up their attack and got onto one '190's tail (Flt Sgt Mulcahy going on). I followed the '190 to the ground, firing at close range and noticing many strikes on the fuselage and bits and pieces flying off the aircraft.

'The '190 then rolled onto its back and almost immediately struck the ground upside down and exploded. About eight more '190s then bounced me from above.

'I left the wreckage blazing fiercely, and escaped by violent evasive action, and everything went forward until over the French coast, where I lost the enemy.

'I claim one Fw 190 destroyed.'

Flt Sgt Mulcahy did not make it home, bailing out 12 miles west of Le Havre. On 18 November the squadron was notified that both he and Plt Off Fraser, downed on 8 September, were being held as PoWs.

The dogfights during the Ramrods were becoming more intense by the day, and on 19 September, whilst flying Ramrod 232, the squadron was attacked by 50 enemy aircraft. They managed to drive away ten, before being set upon by thirty more. Flt Lt J C S Doll destroyed one Fw 190, but losses were inevitable against such overwhelming numbers, and Flg Off

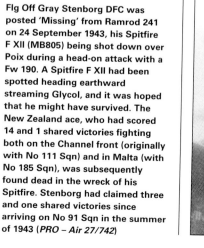

Flg Off Gray Stenborg DFC was posted 'Missing' from Ramrod 241 on 24 September 1943, his Spitfire F XII (MB805) being shot down over Poix during a head-on attack with a Fw 190. A Spitfire F XII had been spotted heading earthward streaming Glycol, and it was hoped that he might have survived. The New Zealand ace, who had scored 14 and 1 shared victories fighting both on the Channel front (originally with No 111 Sqn) and in Malta (with No 185 Sqn), was subsequently found dead in the wreck of his Spitfire. Stenborg had claimed three and one shared victories since arriving on No 91 Sqn in the summer of 1943 (*PRO – Air 27/742*)

Geoffrey Bond, in EN614, failed to return from the sortie. The only hope of finding him came when an aircraft was seen diving into the sea between Furnes and Dunkirk, with German ASR launches heading for the area.

Minutes after Bond's Spitfire had been lost, Flt Sgt Blumer's aircraft (MB799) developed engine trouble, and he was forced to bail out into the sea off Deal. Happily, he was uninjured, and the Australian was quickly rescued by an HSL. There was no trace of his squadronmate, however, and the unit later learned that his body had been recovered from the North Sea by the Germans.

Bond had fallen victim to no less a pilot than the *Gruppenkommandeur* of I./JG 26, Hauptmann Karl Borris, this victory taking his tally to exactly 30. A veteran of the Battle of Britain, Borris remained in charge of the *gruppe* until war's end, by which time his score had risen to 43.

The last week in September was one of the busiest, and most successful, ever for No 91 Sqn. On the 23rd Sqn Ldr Kynaston led the unit on Ramrod 240, escorting 72 Marauders sent to bomb Beauvais airfield. In another successful operation, he and Flt Sgt Blumer shared in the destruction of an Fw 190, Flt Lt Chris Doll destroyed a second, and recently-promoted Flt Lt Stenborg (in MB620) destroyed a Bf 109 and Flt Lt Matthew damaged another Messerschmitt.

The following day the squadron returned to Beauvais on Ramrod 241, and claims were made by Sqn Ldr Kynaston (one Fw 190 destroyed), Flt Lt Doll (one Fw 190 destroyed) and Flt Lt Maridor, in MB849, (one Fw 190 destroyed and one damaged). Sadly, Gray Stenborg, at the controls of F XII MB805, was shot down over Poix in a head-on attack with a Fw 190. A Spitfire F XII was seen heading earthward streaming Glycol, and it was hoped he might have survived. The New Zealand ace, who had scored 14 and 1 shared victories fighting both on the Channel front (originally with No 111 Sqn) and in Malta (with No 185 Sqn), was subsequently found dead in the wreck of his Spitfire.

The 25th was a quieter day for the squadron, but the hectic month ended on the 26th when its pilots went to Beauvais yet again on Ramrod 250. On the return journey Yellow Section found two Bf 109s, which were promptly shot down by Flg Off O'Shaughnessy and his flight commander, Flt Lt Dick Easby, who described the combat on an Intelligence Form 'F', submitted in lieu of a Combat Report:

Flt Lt Dick Easby was OC 'A' Flight for much of 1943 (PRO – Air 27/742)

'I was leading Yellow Section in No 91 Sqn, acting as Escort Cover to Ramrod 250.

'After diving down after two enemy aircraft (and) not being able to close, we turned home on the deck. I observed an aircraft on the starboard side which I, with Yellow 2, turned to investigate. This aircraft proved to be an ME109, which I told Yellow 2 to deal with. Yellow 2 obtained many strikes and the enemy aircraft burst into flames and crashed in a field.

'After Yellow 2 had destroyed his enemy aircraft, we continued on our way. I then observed an ME109 ahead, flying across our track on the deck. I made a quarter attack from the enemy aircraft's starboard side, closing in astern firing. Strikes were seen on the aircraft and debris coming off it. It suddenly pulled up to 500 ft, when on continuing firing the aircraft began to disintegrate, parts falling off and the enemy aircraft burst into flames, and then hit the deck in flames.

'My No 2, Flg Off O'Shaughnessy, confirms this.'

Ramrod 250 ended an incredible month for the unit, which had now scored 99 aerial victories in the war to date. Eighteen of these had been destroyed in September alone, this haul making No 91 Sqn the highest-scoring unit in No 11 Group for that month – indeed, its tally was twice as high as the runner-up!

October began with a move to Tangmere on the 4th, and the pilots soon began working on adding to September's claims. However, it was not until the 18th, and Ramrod 273, that Lt Andrieux (in MB839) destroyed a Fw 190. More success followed 48 hours later on Rodeo 263, which saw the squadron taking part in a fighter sweep of the Beaumont/Bernay area. In a very successful operation, the Tangmere Wing destroyed nine enemy aircraft, of which No 91 Sqn claimed four – Sqn Ldr Kynaston 'bagged' an Fw 190, and Flt Lt Doll, Flg Off Nash and Flt Sgt Blumer each destroyed Bf 109Gs, whilst on the way home the latter pilot sunk a barge on the river Seine and Flg Off Davy shot up a train!

The unit had been so busy with Ramrod work that very few Rhubarbs had been flown. No 91 Sqn had a long tradition of small-scale attacks on opportunist targets, and on 6 November newly-promoted Wt Off Blumer and Flt Sgt R K Fairbairn organised their own operation. They planned a route into northern France and left Tangmere at 1525 hrs. Crossing the French coast at Pont d'Ailly, the pair headed south and damaged a locomotive at Auffray, before turning west. They experienced light, but accurate, flak in the St Victor/Totes area, but continued on to St Ouen, where they destroyed a second locomotive.

Turning north-west, the Spitfires flew on to Gremonville, where they found two trains in a siding. The pilots could not believe their luck, and 'Red' Blumer immediately commenced an attack. Having silenced one flak battery located near the trains, his aircraft (EN626) was hit by a second flak site, and he told Flt Sgt Fairbairn that he would not make it back. His squadronmate last saw him climbing into cloud, with black smoke pouring from the Spitfire's Griffon engine. Fairbairn returned to Tangmere alone, and Wt Off Blumer was posted 'Missing' – a fate he shared with 20 other pilots from the squadron.

By December 1943 No 91 Sqn was top-heavy with experienced pilots, none of whom wished to leave, and it began to attract the attention of Postings Officers looking for potential OTU instructors. All of the pilots

Flg Off Frederick Dash Thomas was killed when his Spitfire F XII EN604 collided with the fighter flown by Flg Off H F Heninger during formation flying practice on 6 December 1943. Thomas's Spitfire crashed near East Grinstead *(PRO – Air 27/742)*

wanted to stay on the squadron, and those with the most operational flying hours desperately tried to hide their Flying Log Books. However, a pilot usually knew when his time was up, for the CO would ask to see him – and his log books! With this threat firmly in mind, 'high-timers' like Flg Offs 'Johnny' Round, Ray Nash, 'Dave' Davy, 'Shag' O'Shaughnessy and 'Wattie' Watterson all kept low profiles as 1943 drew to a close. There was to be no escape for them, however.

'Shag' O'Shaughnessy was the first 'victim', being posted to HQ No 9 Group for Instructor duties on 5 December. He had served on No 91 Sqn since 1 July 1942. 'Johnny' Round was next, being posted to the same unit four days later, with 'Wattie' Watterson leaving on 8 January 1944.

1943 ended with a Ramrod escorting heavy bombers sent to attack secret targets in the Foret de Hesdin, in northern France – the targets were later revealed as V1 rocket launching sites. With these missions taking Spitfires deeper into France than ever before, the squadron had used the 45-gallon drop tanks for the very first time on the 31st. Although they

extended the fighter's range considerably, their use was not without problems, because they often would not jettison when empty, or deliver fuel when full!

The new year began with the loss of Flg Off Harold Heninger on 6 January. He was returning from a bomber escort mission (in EN223) to the Rouen area with 13-kill Malta ace Flg Off 'Paddy' Schade DFM when they both suffered engine problems. Turning for home, Canadian Heninger was forced to bail out before crossing the French coast, but his parachute streamed and he fell to his death.

On a more positive note, Lt Andrieux claimed his fourth kill the very next day when the squadron escorted Mosquito fighter-bombers sent to attack targets in Embroy. The Frenchman downed one of two Fw 190s found patrolling at very low-level ten miles east of Berck.

On 23 January the squadron flew Ramrod 472, escorting four waves of 54 Marauders attacking targets in the St Omer area. The mission was successful, but Flt Sgt J H Hymas – flying Spitfire MB832 – did not return to

The Heninger brothers, Ray (left) and Harold (right), both served with No 91 Sqn during 1943. Harold Heninger was posted 'Missing' from a Ramrod to the Rouen area on 6 January 1944, his Spitfire suffering chronic engine failure over enemy territory. Heninger bailed out and was made a PoW

Spitfire F XII MB832 is seen soon after it had suffered a catastrophic landing accident at Hamble on 6 June 1943 – no specific details pertaining to this incident have yet been found. First flown by Jean Maridor on an Air Test on 22 May 1943 (then coded 'DL-S'), MB832 was used by the French ace to destroy an Fw 190 off Folkestone three days later. He continued to fly it until this accident occurred, but it is uncertain whether he was at the controls when the fighter was all but written off. MB832 had only been issued to No 91 Sqn from the production line at High Post Aerodrome exactly three weeks earlier. Sent to Air Service Training for a total rebuild, it did not return to the squadron until 3 January 1944. This time it lasted just 20 days, being lost on the 23rd when Flt Sgt J H Hymas was downed by German fighters on Ramrod 472. MB832 had flown for only 28.30 hours (*via Andy Thomas*)

Tangmere. He was seen shortly after crossing the French coast on his way home, but then nothing more was heard from him on the radio. It was later learned that he had been captured and was being held as a PoW.

On the same day, Flg Off Cameron McNeil was flying Spitfire EN624 on a practice bombing mission over Pagham Harbour, in Sussex, when he turned steeply to observe the fall of his bombs, stalled and fatally crashed. This aircraft had long been known amongst the squadron's pilots as a 'rogue' Spitfire, and it had been returned to the RAF's testing and evaluation establishment at Boscombe Down following complaints that it always flew with its left wing down. The problem was traced to distorted control cables, which were replaced before the aircraft was reissued to No 91 Sqn.

Poor weather was always a problem for air operations in the early months of the year, and on 31 January the squadron was flying Ramrod 500 (escorting Mosquitos to Dieppe) when it encountered a storm front before crossing the French coast. Told to return to base, Sqn Ldr Kynaston had just ordered a gentle turn to port when Flg Off Derek Inskip, flying Spitfire EN613, and Flt Sgt Robert Fairbairn, in Spitfire EN618, collided. Inskip's aircraft dived straight into the sea, but Flt Sgt Fairbairn pulled up into cloud and said he would have to bail out. He gave a fix for ASR launches, but ten seconds later dived out of the cloud and into the sea. The squadron and other aircraft circled the area, but nothing was seen apart from two patches of oil and foam on the water.

SPITFIRE F XIV ARRIVES

At the end of February the squadron was notified that it was going to be the second unit to convert to the latest mark of Spitfire, the F XIV. Powered by a 2035-hp Rolls-Royce Griffon 65 engine, the aircraft was better than the F XII in all aspects of its performance. No 91 Sqn duly departed Tangmere for RAF Castle Camps, in Essex, where the conversion would take place, on 29 February.

The unit's pilots and groundcrews worked hard to get to grips with their new Spitfire F XIVs, and by 7 March they were ready to rejoin the fight. Their hopes were cruelly dashed, however, when they found out that they were being sent to RAF Drem, east of Edinburgh! Despite the journey north being hampered by very poor weather, No 91 Sqn began exercising with the new aircraft from the Scottish base on the 8th.

On 12 March Flt Sgts Sayer and Ritchie were scrambled to assist a Liberator bomber struggling to reach its base, which they did successfully. Nothing more was heard from Charles Sayer, however, until the unit was informed that a Spitfire had crashed near RAF Turnhouse. The fighter proved to be Sayer's RB172, and it had buried itself deep in the ground. Initially, no trace could be found of the pilot, but the sad news came through the next day that his body had been discovered in the cockpit.

By this time the squadron was becoming restless. The traditional occupation of No 91 Sqn was attacking Germans, and they had been away from the action for nearly a month. It was to be another month, though, before the pilots' prayers were answered, and they were ordered south to West Malling – firmly back in No 11 Group territory!

The unit's new home was famous as a nightfighter base, and its operations were divided between night flying, carried out by resident Mosquito squadrons (Nos 85 and 96) and daylight sweeps performed by at least one Spitfire squadron – No 91 Sqn replaced No 616 Sqn, equipped with Spitfire HF VIIs. The squadron soon settled into the comfortable surroundings of the Kentish fighter station.

Within 48 hours of arriving, five-kill ace Flt Lt J C S 'Chris' Doll was given the chance to show just what the new Spitfire F XIV could do in combat when he was scrambled to 40,000 ft to intercept two Fw 190s. As he got closer to the fighters, he was forced to climb even higher, reaching an altitude of 44,500 ft. Wounded in the brief combat which followed, Doll passed out, only regaining consciousness as the fighter dived through 7000 ft. He just had time to crash-land, and subsequently spent some weeks in hospital recovering.

Air Vice-Marshal J B Cole Hamilton, AOC No 85 Group, presents French ace Flg Off Jacques 'Jaco' Andrieux with the DFC at West Malling on 9 May 1944 *(Sqn Ldr Nash)*

All of No 91 Sqn's pilots gather for a photograph, taken at West Malling on 9 May 1944. They are, from left to right, Elcock, Brown, Nash, Balcombe, Bond, Maridor, unknown, Smith, Andrieux, McKay, Kynaston, Cruickshank, Costello, Schade, Huntley, Oxspring (Wing Leader No 24 Wing), unknown, unknown *(W Taylor)*

On 28 April the F XIV was finally given the all-clear to operate over enemy territory, allowing Flg Offs H D Johnson and A R Cruickshank to be vectored onto an 'enemy' aircraft detected over Rouen – this proved to be an American Lockheed Lightning!

Whilst at Drem, the squadron had practised flying the F XIV at night. With previous marks of Spitfire, the glare from the exhaust stubs had always ruined pilots' night vision, but the F XIV did not suffer from this problem, and the squadron continued to fly occasional night patrols from West Malling.

Whilst performing one such sortie, on 29 April, Flg Off John Collis (in Spitfire RB187) became separated from his leader in cloud. His leader called and Collis replied, saying he was alright, but nothing more was heard from him, and he did not return to West Malling. A later search found some wreckage in the water off North Foreland, but the sea was too rough for the ASR Walrus to land. Collis was duly posted 'Missing'.

On 9 May Air Vice-Marshal Cole Hamilton, AOC No 85 Group, visited West Malling and presented Lt Andrieux with the DFC. The Frenchman was both a popular officer and a superb pilot, and the award was well deserved, but he was not one to rest on his laurels.

On 14 May he went on a shipping recce with Plt Off J Monihan. Finding no worthwhile targets, they flew on to Flushing where, at very low level, they attacked an 800-2000 ton ship of the *Sperrbrucher* class. Having badly damaged the vessel, they returned to West Malling in a jubilant mood, only to be told by the CO that 'a Rhubarb was a piece of cake, but a shipping attack in that area was bloody silly'! The following day, Andrieux did carry out a Rhubarb, and near the French coast he shot up a black Renault staff car, hitting three Luftwaffe aircrew who jumped out of it. A few more Rhubarbs were completed, but poor weather prevented flying for much of the month, greatly disappointing the squadron, which was looking forward to carrying out fighter sweeps over France (the F XIVs were fitted with 90-gallon drop tanks, which greatly extended their range).

With extensive troop movements all over southern England, it was obvious that the invasion of 'Fortress Europe' was imminent, and on 5 June black and white 'invasion stripes' were painted on all squadron aircraft. The D-Day landings took place the following day, and No 91 Sqn was heavily committed to supporting the invasion forces, and flying defensive patrols.

Australian pilot Wt Off 'Red' Blumer returned to No 91 Sqn on 8 June 1944, having evaded capture for more than six months. He had been shot down by flak whilst attacking trains near Gremonville on 6 November 1943, Blumer force-landing in F XII EN626 'DL-E' near Rouen. And although he escaped capture, his intact Spitfire did not. As the first example of an intact Griffon-engined fighter to fall into enemy hands, EN626 was closely examined by Luftwaffe engineers. Restored to airworthiness, it was first flown at the Rechlin test centre, before being passed on to 2. *Staffel Versuchsverband Oberkommando der Luftwaffe* (2nd Flight of the Luftwaffe HQ Trials Unit). Its ultimate fate remains unknown *(A G Blumer)*

NEW AIRCRAFT, NEW ROLE

That same day highly-experienced Belgian fighter pilot Flt Lt Eugene Seghers DFC arrived on the squadron from HQ Air Defence Great Britain. A veteran of the *Blitzkrieg* of 1940 (with the Belgian Air Force) and the Battle of Britain, he had completed three operational tours on the Channel Front, and his combat experience was to be put to good use during his brief time with No 91 Sqn.

As with most Allied fighter units, No 91 Sqn saw no enemy aircraft during the first 48 hours of the invasion, although on the 7th a formation of six aircraft was intercepted over the Straits of Dover. These were quickly identified as being P-47s, although the American pilots initially failed to spot that their 'opponents' were Spitfires, and two of them fired short bursts at the RAF fighters before realising their error – fortunately their aim was poor.

On 8 June, much to everyone's surprise, Wt Off 'Red' Blumer arrived back on the squadron, having been posted 'Missing' on 6 November 1943. He had been shot down by flak near Evreux and duly picked up by the resistance movement. Hidden by them, he then escaped into Switzerland by swimming across a semi-frozen river. Blumer arrived on the other side in a terrible state, where he was found by an elderly gentleman, who took him in.

The Australian decided that he did not want to be interned, so he spirited himself back across the border into France and re-established contact with the resistance. A plan for his escape was formulated, but it was clear that a man with bright golden hair and a ruddy complexion was not going to pass unnoticed through southern France! The answer was simple, though, and with his hair dyed black, 'Monsieur' Blumer successfully reached Spain!

Having crossed the Pyrenees, he was arrested and briefly interned, before returning to England via Gibraltar. Blumer's arrival on the squadron was completely unannounced, and it seemed that he had not bothered to tell anyone in authority of his return! His personal appearance was also something to behold, with his black hair and bright golden roots!

'Red' Blumer could not have timed his return to No 91 Sqn better, for the unit was about to enter the most hectic period in its brief history.

93

'DIVER'!

As early as 22 April 1944, the Royal Observer Corps posts around the southern coast of England had been warned of possible attacks by pilotless aircraft launched from the Pas de Calais and Cherbourg peninsular areas. The code name for sighting one of these aircraft was 'Diver', which was also the name most widely used by the RAF. However, to the civilians on the receiving end, and the popular press, they soon became known as 'flying bombs', 'buzz bombs' or 'doodlebugs'.

Whatever name was used, one thing was clear. The weapon brought terror of an entirely new kind to London and the southern counties of England – counties that were only just recovering from the devastating *Blitz* and the *Baedecker* raids of 1941/42.

The V1, or *Vergeltungswaffe* (revenge weapon) 1, was a pilotless mid-wing monoplane with a wingspan of 17 ft 6 in and an overall length of 25 ft 4.5 in. It was constructed largely of thin sheet steel and plywood, and was propelled by a pulse jet engine. The weapon was armed with a warhead containing 850 kg of high explosive, and its direction, altitude and range were all controlled by a gyroscope, housed in the tail unit.

The performance of the V1 was to cause enormous problems for Air Defence of Great Britain (ADGB), as Fighter Command had temporarily been renamed from the outset of the campaign. The weapons flew at speeds between 300 and 420 mph, with an average of 350 mph. Their altitude varied from tree-top height to a maximum of 8000 ft, with an average of 3000 to 4000 ft. The maximum effective range of the V1 was 130 miles, and a typical flight lasted between 20 and 25 minutes.

The aircraft required to counter the V1 threat needed excellent performance, especially at low altitude, and sufficient firepower to ensure that as many V1s as possible were destroyed in the air, rather than exploding on the ground. Fortunately, No 91 Sqn, flying the Spitfire F XIV and based at West Malling (almost in the centre of most V1 flight paths), was ideally equipped and located to take on the V1 menace.

At 0408 hrs on Tuesday, 13 June, Royal Observer Corps observation post Mike 2, housed in a Napoleonic War Martello tower at Dymchurch, on the Kent coast, spotted the first 'Diver' heading for London. Four aircraft of No 91 Sqn were scrambled just after dawn to intercept the pilotless bomb, and the four others launched soon after it. They were unable to intercept them, however, and the last one crashed harmlessly into farmland at Platt, not far from West Malling. The V1, described in the squadron diary as 'a bomb affair with wings and a rudder, and a jet contraption for propulsion', was a very worrying development for the squadron, with particular concerns regarding tactics, and the likely methods of actually destroying the rockets in the air.

Fortunately, a defensive plan had been drawn up by senior officers in ADGB HQ some months earlier, and this was put into immediate effect. The priority was to defend London, and a thick balloon barrage was erected around the capital and a belt of anti aircraft guns situated on the North Downs. The initial plan was that the fighter aircraft would operate with complete freedom south of the gun belt, and at first the plan worked well.

The squadron was immediately deployed on 'Diver' patrols, and on 16 June Canadian Flt Lt H Bruce Moffett, flying Spitfire RM617, destroyed the unit's first 'Diver' (also the first for a West Malling squadron). Spitfire F XIVs had been scrambled against a 'Diver' coming in over Dungeness, taking off from West Malling at 1035 hrs. Moffett intercepted the V1 over Tonbridge, and then chased it for over 20 miles until he eventually shot it down in the Redhill area. The squadron was jubilant, and amid the celebrations, advice on destroying 'Divers' was 'freely available from Bruce Moffett – an old and experienced hand'!

The squadron, in common with other ADGB units, was still committed to flying defensive patrols in support of the invasion, but such was the 'Diver' threat that all such patrols were suspended from 17 June. That same day saw three 'Divers' destroyed, followed by ten 24 hours later – including two by the CO and four (three shared) by Ray Nash (in RB169). On 19 June it was confirmed that No 91 Sqn would be engaged on 'Diver' patrols only until further notice, and four more were destroyed, including one by Bruce Moffett (in NH701) which exploded and knocked off his propeller tip – the first damage of the campaign.

By this time 'Divers' were being launched in increasing numbers, and the defensive system had degenerated into a dangerous free for all between guns, barrage balloons and fighters of all types. It was extremely hazardous for all concerned, especially the civilian population, and the plan was revised with effect from 21 June.

In good visibility the fighters would have complete freedom of action, with no guns operating (code name 'Flabby'). In poor visibility no fighters would operate and the guns would have complete freedom of action (code name 'Spouse'). Code name 'Fickle' was the dubious mixture of fighters, guns and balloons. The light anti-aircraft guns could engage visual targets, while the balloons could operate up to 8000 feet, with fighters also being permitted to enter the gun belt to make visual interceptions.

The new plan meant that the role of West Malling's Mosquito nightfighter squadrons (Nos 29, 96 and 409) was considerably reduced, and so they were all redeployed on 19/20 June (to Hunsdon, Ford and Hunsdon respectively). The nightfighters were replaced at West Malling by three Spitfire squadrons, namely No 41 Sqn – No 91's 'old friends' from the Tangmere Wing – still flying the Spitfire F XII, the Dutchmen of No 322 Sqn, equipped with Spitfire F XIVs and No 610 Sqn, also operating F XIVs.

23 June saw a remarkable piece of flying by Flg Off Ken Collier RAAF, which also brought into effect a new method of destroying 'Divers'. Flying Spitfire NH698, Collier took off from West Malling at 2150 hrs and commenced a 'Diver' patrol along the south coast. Approaching Beachy Head at 2240 hrs, he spotted a V1 which had just crossed the coast, flying at 330 mph at a height of 2500 ft. The subsequent Consolidated 'Diver' Combat Report, submitted to HQ ADGB, described the action thus:

'"Diver" sighted over Beachy. Strikes seen from bursts fired with no effect. Pilot ran out of ammunition, and being close behind, overtook "Diver", formated alongside and, with wing, tipped it over on second attempt. "Diver" spun in and exploded when hitting ground.'

On 23 June 1944 Flg Off Ken Collier became the first pilot to 'tip' a V1 with the wing of his aircraft (Spitfire F XIV NH698). The centre of much press coverage for this extraordinary exploit, the Australian pilot claimed seven V1s destroyed between 22 June and 29 July. He continued serving with the squadron until his death in action on 5 December 1944 *(Author's collection)*

The squadron diarist, in his own inimitable way, also recorded the events of the evening:

'Collier's effort was a clear case of determination crowned at the last moment with success. He came across this particular "Diver" just after it had crossed over Beachy, and immediately gave chase. Getting within range, he fired, with no apparent effect as it carried straight on. This peeved him somewhat, so he had another go, and in fact several goes, but still nothing happened, and what was worse he ran clean out of ammo.

'By this time Ken was really swearing mad, and was determined to do or die. He therefore formated with it, and with his wing, tipped it over. On his second attempt down it went in a tight spin, but it very nearly landed in the centre of a town. However, it did no damage, and Flg Off Collier thus brought into practice a new method of getting rid of these flying bombs.'

This method of destroying 'Divers' became famous, and widely used, especially over the sea. Although it was safer for pilots because there was no danger from the effects of the exploding V1, its use over built-up areas was highly questionable, and there were also concerns later in the campaign that the Germans had fitted some V1s with explosive devices to prevent 'tipping'.

25 June brought bad weather, which curtailed flying for much of the day. A few 'Diver' patrols were flown late on though, the last of these being conducted by Frenchman Lt Henri de Bordas (in NH654) and Wt Off Blumer. They left West Malling at 2230 hrs, heading south over the

Weald of Kent to a patrol line between Ashford and Tenterden. At 2305 hrs de Bordas destroyed a 'Diver' near Woodchurch, and the pair turned for home. Blumer landed at Staplehurst Advanced Landing Ground (ALG) to refuel, before taking off once again, in poor weather, for the short flight to West Malling.

At about 2330 hrs, for no apparent reason, his Spitfire (RM617) dived straight into the ground at Nettlestead, just short of West Malling's runway, and 'Red' Blumer was killed. After all his exploits with No 91 Sqn in 1943, and his amazing escape from France, it was tragic that he should die in a flying accident, the cause of which was never determined.

The weather improved on the 27th and six 'Divers' were destroyed, including one shared by supernumerary squadron leader Peter Bond (in RB161) and Canadian Flg Off R A McPhie. They chased the V1 right over West Malling before finally bringing it down just north of the airfield boundary. The exact location was confirmed by the Station Commander, Wg Cdr John O'Neill DFC, who lived at Offham House, and whose windows it had just blown in!

The West Malling squadrons enjoyed a great rivalry with Hawker Tempest V-equipped No 150 Wing at Newchurch, on Romney Marsh. By 29 June the Tempest Wing led the West Malling squadrons in terms of the number of 'Divers' it had destroyed, but it was universally agreed (at West Malling at least!) that Ray Nash had evened the score somewhat by destroying a 'Diver' which crashed on Newchurch's perimeter track! The squadron ended this day exhausted, having flown a total of 66 hours and 15 minutes – a record daily total since formation.

The month ended with the destruction of four 'Divers', including the fourth destroyed by Flt Lt Maridor. The total downed for the month was 63, and the squadron had flown 1049 hours – a record monthly total.

Flg Off McPhie, Flg Off Ettles, Sqn Ldr Bond and Flt Lt Johnson relax between sorties at West Malling during the summer of 1944 – stood behind them is LAC 'Nobby' Staines. The squadron's dispersal hut had only recently been vacated by Mosquito nightfighter-equipped No 85 Sqn, hence the latter unit's distinctive white hexagon marking on its wall *(via M Llewellyn)*

Two of the No 91 Sqn's 'Diver' aces –
Flg Off Ted Topham (9 and 1 shared
V1s destroyed) and Flt Lt Ray Nash
(17 and 3 shared V1s destroyed) are
debriefed at West Malling by the
squadron Intelligence Officer, Flg Off
Kember. Ted Topham appears to
have acquired the lifejacket
belonging to fellow New Zealander,
Flt Lt Alex Smith
(Author's collection)

July opened with six 'Divers' being destroyed (including two by Sqn Ldr Kynaston) on the 1st. Three days later Flg Off McPhie was married, Flt Lt Maridor was engaged to a WAAF officer at West Malling, and a photographer arrived from HQ ADGB to photograph 'the prize Spitfire squadron engaged on "Diver" work'.

The V1 claims continued to rise, with seven on the 3rd, seven on the 4th and six on the 5th. After a claimless day on the 6th, the squadron enjoyed their best 24-hour period of the campaign on the 7th when no less than 12 were destroyed – Sqn Ldr Kynaston and Flg Offs William Marshall, A R Cruickshank and H M Neil all destroyed two each.

On 9 July personnel on the ground at West Malling were alarmed to see Canadian Flt Lt J W P Draper DFC (a veteran of the North African campaign, who had joined the squadron on 14 June having already claimed four and one shared aircraft destroyed) flying over the airfield blazing away at a 'Diver' with his cannons from just 100 yards astern. Fortunately for everyone on the ground, one of his guns was unserviceable and he missed! Draper went on to successfully destroy six 'Divers'.

At 2206 hrs that same day, Flg Off Marshall (in NH701) shot down a 'Diver' just north of Dungeness. To his horror he saw that it was gliding straight towards the town of Lydd, and so he closed to less than 50 yards and fired again. The V1 exploded in mid air, without a doubt saving many lives, but nearly blowing Bill Marshall up in the process!

Left and above
Flt Lt 'Johnny' Johnson poses with his Spitfire F XIV (RB188) at West Malling during July 1944. This aircraft carried one of the few photographically-documented examples of nose-art applied to Griffon-engined Spitfires, being christened *BRÜMHILDE* and adorned with a V1-riding red-head! 'Johnny' Johnson (13 and 1 shared V1s destroyed – five of these were claimed with RB188) joined No 91 Sqn in 1942, and remained with the unit until 1946. RB188 had been issued to No 91 Sqn on 29 February 1944, but was returned to Air Service Training for modifications on 5 May. Once back with No 91 Sqn, it was extensively used during the 'Diver' campaign largely by Flt Lt Johnson, although claims were also made by Flt Sgt Geoff Kay (1 shared), Flg Off Ken Collier (1) and Flt Lt Jean Maridor (1). Leaving No 91 Sqn on 9 August 1944, RB188 was issued firstly to No 130 Sqn and then No 350 Sqn. On 11 February 1945 it crashed in poor weather near Turnhouse, killing the pilot, Flt Sgt Ritchie. Repaired at Air Service Training, RB188 was sold to Vickers-Armstrongs on 10 May 1950, who subsequently supplied it to the Royal Thai Air Force as U14-18/93 (*both photographs via Sqn Ldr Johnson*)

As the Allied advance in France, and continual round the clock bombing, began to affect the V1 launch sites, so the numbers of 'Divers' decreased in the early days of July. From the 12th to the 19th, the squadron only accounted for 11 flying bombs despite an intense pattern of patrols. Although the numbers of V1s launched had decreased, it was clear that too many were still reaching London, and on 17 July the defensive plan was altered once again.

The previous code names were abandoned, but the key development was the movement of all guns from inland positions to a coastal gun belt between St Margarets Bay, near Dover, and Cuckmere Haven, in Sussex. The guns enjoyed complete freedom of fire within the belt at all times and in all conditions. The fighters enjoyed freedom of action forward of the gun belt (i.e. over the Channel), and between it and the strengthened balloon barrage further inland. The effect of the change in tactics was immediately apparent, and many lives were saved by it.

ADGB HQ decided to move Nos 91 and 322 Sqns forward into the coastal gun belt, and on 20 July the unit was notified of the move to Deanland ALG, four miles west of Hailsham, in Sussex. Upon receiving this news, Flg Off G C McKay carried out a recce and found that Deanland was a typical ALG, with four 'blister' hangars and tented accommodation. After the wonderful luxury of West Malling this was terrible news, and he concluded his report by saying it was 'the last place on earth any sane man would go to'! The move was made the next day, however, and the squadrons' pilots mourned their departure from West Malling by drinking 'vast quantities of ale' at Hilden Manor!

With the move to Deanland came a slight increase in 'Diver' claims, but not to the levels enjoyed earlier in the campaign. On 30 July two were destroyed, including one by Sqn Ldr Bond, who 'had the indecency to shoot one down within half-a-mile of the aerodrome – too close, was the general consensus of opinion'!

Given the potentially lethal mixture of V1s, fighters of all types, guns and balloons, it was remarkable how few casualties the squadron suffered in the 'Diver' campaign. Sadly, though, July ended with the loss of two

Two good friends and a Spitfire F XIV, probably photographed at Deanland in 1944. Yorkshireman Flt Sgt Geoff Kay and Lancastrian Wt Off Freddie Lewis pose with their specially-customised 'Mae Wests' – Kay's boasts a white rose and Lewis's a red one! Subsequently promoted to flying officer, Geoffrey Kay lost his life on 12 May 1945 when he hit the ground at RAF Ludham while practising aerobatics in Spitfire F XXI LA200 *(F A Lewis)*

A rare photograph of a No 91 Sqn Spitfire F XIV, which reveals the extensive 'invasion' striping that was applied to all aircraft assigned to the unit on the eve of the D-Day landings. These stripes were hastily applied by hand at Deanland, hence their unevenness in appearance. Very few photos of 'Nigeria' Squadron F XIVs have come to light over the years

very experienced pilots – Flt Lt 'Gin' Seghers and Flg Off 'Paddy' Schade. At 1420 hrs on 26 July, Belgian veteran Seghers collided with a 'Diver' over Uckfield, in Sussex, his Spitfire (RM743) blowing up and the wreckage falling west of East Hoathley.

Five days later, whilst flying in poor visibility, 'Paddy' Schade (in RM654) collided with a Tempest V (EJ586) flown by Flt Sgt A A Wilson of No 486 'New Zealand' Sqn. The aircraft crashed north of Bexhill and both pilots were killed. The loss of two such experienced aviators marred what had been an excellent month for the squadron, with 104 'Divers' destroyed.

The poor weather continued until 2 August, but improved again the next day as Flt Lt Jean Maridor and Section Officer Jean Lambourn were finalising their wedding plans. The Frenchman was still flying operationally, though, and at 1245 hrs he intercepted a 'Diver' over Rolvenden, in Kent. He fired a burst at it, but the V1 did not explode. Instead, it glided down towards Benenden School, which at that time housed a large military hospital.

Maridor dived down after it and, at very close range, he opened fire again. The 'Diver' exploded, preventing what would have been an enormous loss of life, but the blast blew off the Spitfire's wing. The aircraft (RM656) fell beside a lake in the grounds of the school, and 'Mari', as he was known on the squadron, was killed – eight days before he was due to be married. The action was witnessed by many people on the ground, and it was their opinion that Maridor had deliberately fired again, knowing that he stood little or no chance of surviving.

Jean Maridor had served on No 91 Sqn since 14 February 1942, and was much admired by all who knew him. He had destroyed at least four enemy aircraft in the air, as well as 11 V1s, and was one of the squadron's anti-shipping experts. From 18 January until 19 March 1944 he had served with No 61 OTU at RAF Rednall, but that was his only break from frontline flying since joining No 615 Sqn in the autumn of 1941. Maridor

Flt Lt Jean Maridor and his fiancee, Section Officer Jean Lambourn, are seen together soon after announcing their engagement in the spring of 1944. Tragically, the French ace was to lose his life attacking a V1 just eight days before he was due to be married (*J Holme*)

harboured a fanatical hatred of the Germans following the occupation of his homeland, and it was particularly sad that France was on the verge of total liberation when he was killed.

The 'Diver' campaign was almost over as August began. On the 5th, 'Paddy' Schade was buried at Uxbridge, and three days later Jean Maridor was laid to rest at Brookwood. At the latter pilot's funeral there was a graveside presentation of the *Legion d'Honneur* by General Valin, C-in-C of the Free French Air Force, and the service was attended by many RAF and Free French officers.

The funerals of two such experienced fighter pilots provided a sad ending to No 91 Sqn's 'Diver' campaign – a campaign in which they had been so successful. The squadron was released from 'Diver' operations on 9 August, having officially destroyed a total of 185 flying bombs (unofficially, this figure may have been as high as 189). This was the highest tally scored by a Spitfire squadron, and the third highest overall, beaten only by Nos 3 (288 officially and 305.5 unofficially) and 486 Sqns (223 officially and 241 unofficially) from the Newchurch Tempest Wing.

MORE RAMRODS, RODEOS & RHUBARBS

On 9 August 1944 No 91 Sqn flew its Spitfire F XIVs to Hawkinge and exchanged them for the LF IXs of No 402 'Canadian' Sqn. The pilots were disappointed to lose the superb Griffon Spitfires, but were pleased to be back on the offensive again, flying Ramrods, Rodeos and Rhubarbs. There was also the possibility of going over to France, as control of the squadron had been transferred to the 2nd Tactical Air Force (TAF) from ADGB.

The handling characteristics and performance of the Merlin-engined Spitfire IX were quite different to those of the Griffon-engined Spitfire F XIV, and as some No 91 Sqn pilots had not previously flown the former type, all aircrew carried out a one-hour familiarisation flight.

There was little respite for the squadron after this brief training period, because on 14 August it flew Ramrod 1199, escorting 670 Lancasters and Halifaxes to the Falaise area. Operations continued the next day with Rodeo 381, which saw the unit participate in a wing-strength fighter sweep of the Brussels, St Trond, Charleroi and Cambrai areas.

With the sweep almost over, No 91 Sqn attacked an enemy troop convoy north of the Somme. Greeted by intense light arms fire, the pilots pressed home their strafing runs and Sqn Ldr Norman Kynaston's Spitfire (MK909) was hit by flak, forcing him to bail out 12 miles from the French coast. An extensive ASR search was mounted the next day, but no trace of

Spitfire LF IX MK734 is seen at Manston in the autumn of 1944. This aircraft was flown on seven sorties by Plt Off Fred Lewis, who was undertaking his second tour with No 91 Sqn. Initially issued to No 56 Sqn, MK734 had been involved in a taxying collision with NH152 at Newchurch ALG on 21 May 1944. Following repair, it was sent to No 402 'Canadian' Sqn (hence the maple leaf marking below the cockpit) on 17 July, and then to No 91 Sqn on 9 August 1944. The aircraft was damaged again on 15 March 1945, and following rectification it was issued to No 326 'French' Sqn, before being transferred to the *Armée de l'Air* post-war (*via* E B Morgan)

the squadron CO was found, although a dinghy and occupant had been spotted, and then lost again, in deteriorating visibility.

Norman Kynaston had been a popular CO, having served on No 91 Sqn since 18 November 1942. Always in the thick of the action, and usually leading from the front, he had scored four and one shared victories against manned aircraft, and claimed 17 V1s destroyed – all whilst serving as commanding officer of the 'Nigeria' Squadron. Awarded a DFC in October 1943, Kynaston posthumously received a Bar to this decoration in September 1944. He would be a very hard act to follow.

No 91 Sqn's new CO was pre-war officer Sqn Ldr Peter Bond, who had joined the unit as a supernumerary in the summer and claimed ten V1s destroyed during the 'Diver' campaign.

From the 17 to 26 September, No 91 Sqn was heavily involved in Operation *Market*, which was the airborne phase of Operation *Market Garden* – better known as the ill-fated Arnhem landings. The squadron began by escorting the Northern Force, with their troop-carrying Horsa gliders, to the drop zone. This operation was plagued by bad luck and poor planning, and the mission began to unravel almost immediately when a glider landed in the sea. Two of the squadron's Spitfires orbited the ditched Horsa until help arrived.

A pre-war RAF officer, Peter Bond arrived on No 91 Sqn on 5 February 1944 as a supernumerary squadron leader – details of his wartime service up until then have not been discovered. He assumed command of the unit on 15 August 1944 following the death of Sqn Ldr Kynaston, and remained in the post until 1 March 1945. Bond was subsequently killed, as a wing commander, on 30 September 1946 in a Hornet F 1 when he flew into a hill in Wales in cloud. This photograph of Peter Bond was taken at Manston in early 1945 (*Penelope Maskill-Bourke*)

A great many sorties were flown by No 91 Sqn over the next few days, pilots escorting troop-carrying Dakotas and, as the battle wore on, transport aircraft dropping supplies. On 26 September the unit escorted 36 Dakotas to and from the airstrip at Grave, near Nijmegen. The briefing for the operation was held at Deanland, and was attended by Princess Juliana of the Netherlands. The Wing Leader, ex-No 91 Sqn CO Wg Cdr 'Bobby' Oxspring, 'put up a colossal black' by telling the pilots, in the presence of the Princess, that 'Press tits time was at -'. Not content with that, he continued, telling the Dutch pilots of No 322 Sqn to pay particular attention to 'Press tits time'! Undaunted by this, the Princess stayed for lunch and tea in the mess tent.

The squadron was based at Biggin Hill from 17 until 29 October, when it moved to Manston. It was said that one of the primary reasons for the move was that the Station Commander at the former base did not want scruffy No 91 Sqn on his station – unit personnel had been living in tents since 21 July!

Few operations were flown from Biggin Hill due to poor weather, but the squadron did participate in Ramrod 1349 on 28 October, escorting 250 Lancasters to Walcheren. Sqn Ldr George Reid RCAF, flying with the unit as a supernumerary in Spitfire MK453, was posted 'Missing' from this operation, which was plagued by poor weather.

Following its move to Manston, No 91 Sqn began to fly Ramrods deeper into Germany as the Allied advance progressed relentlessly eastwards. The bomber escort missions continued throughout November, although they were often hampered by poor weather.

On the 21st of the month Flt Lt Ray Nash DFC left the squadron for No 61 OTU, where he would serve as an instructor. He had managed to avoid the Postings Officer for several months after the conclusion of the anti-'Diver' campaign, although he was finally caught after more than two years of flying with No 91 Sqn! The 20-kill V1 ace (who had also been involved in the destruction of three fighters) was long overdue a rest, yet he managed to return to operational flying as CO of No 1 Sqn in April 1945. Nash, who had often led No 91 Sqn into battle during the summer and autumn of 1944, was replaced on 'B' Flight by Flt Lt G H Huntley.

The Ramrods continued into December, and on the 5th the squadron escorted Lancasters returning from a raid on Hamm. Whilst en route to the rendezvous point, a force of 100+ Fw 190s and Bf 109s was seen flying in two boxes at 18,000 ft north-east of Wesel. An intense dogfight ensued, which was subsequently described by the squadron Intelligence Officer, Flg Off Kember, in his report compiled for HQ, Fighter Command:

'An engagement took place in which three ME109s were destroyed and one ME109 damaged. A further ME109 was seen to go down in flames. There is a probability that this was shot down by Flg Off K Collier, who is missing from this operation, although at present there is no concrete evidence to support this claim.

'Flt Lt W C Marshall (Claim: two ME109s destroyed), stated:

'"I was Yellow 1 flying out to meet the bombers on Ramrod 1394, and about seven minutes from the R/V (1135hrs) I sighted two boxes of about 50 aircraft each, which I recognised as FW190s and ME109s mixed in each formation. They saw us immediately and pulled round to meet us on a head-on attack in which I did not fire. After they had passed through us

I pulled up into sun, jettisoned my drop tank and dived back into the gaggle. I got on to the tail of a section of four ME109s flying in close formation line astern and I fired at No 1 of this section from astern at 200/250 yards as I dived down on them. I did not see strikes on this aircraft, but at that moment Nos 2 and 3 collided and broke up in the air. I did not see the pilots bail out. The other two dived to the deck. I climbed back up to 18,000 ft, not seeing any other aircraft till I was bounced by 50+ FW190s when I dived for the deck and came home.

'"I claim two ME109s destroyed. My camera was not switched on."

'Flg Off J A Faulkner (Claim: one ME109 destroyed) reported:
'"I was flying as Yellow 2 on Ramrod 1394 flying to rendezvous with bombers. About seven minutes before R/V Yellow 1 reported aircraft, where I saw two boxes of 50 each at two o'clock. I watched these as they swung round to six o'clock, and we turned to meet them head on. As they approached I recognised them as FW190s, and immediately after that they fired at Yellow Section. As they went by I pulled up into sun, jettisoned my drop tank and did a counter attack on the last aircraft of the leading box, which was an ME109. At about 600 yards' range he broke to starboard and I gave him a short burst, following him round as he dived through the second box. He then pulled up and flew straight and level. I closed in to about 50 yards' range and opened fire with a short burst as I closed rapidly on him.

'"I saw strikes all along the starboard wing and pieces flew off. He flicked over onto his back and spun down with pieces falling off. I saw him explode on the ground. The pilot did not bail out. This was witnessed by Plt Off F A Lewis.

'"A second ME109 dived across in front of me and I dived after him, but on looking behind me I saw eight ME109s coming out of the sun to attack me, and as I broke round the first two opened fire. As I could not attack any of them without being bounced by others, I broke off into cloud and returned to base.

'"I claim one ME109 destroyed."

'Plt Off F A Lewis recounted:
'"In the area where the above combat occurred I saw an ME109 being attacked by a Spitfire, who obtained cannon strikes on the centre of the fuselage, upon which the tail fell off the enemy aircraft and it fell away and burst into flames on the way down. The time of this combat was 1135 hrs."

'Flt Lt E Topham (Claim: one ME109 damaged), stated:
'"I was flying Blue 4 on Ramrod 1394, and on nearing R/V I heard Yellow 1 call over the R/T that FW190s were approaching. Blue Section broke into sun and I saw 50+ FW190s and ME109s mixed in one box and a further number below them. Blue 3 broke immediately into the leading section, by which time I had jettisoned my drop tank and followed him. We chased one FW190 followed by two ME109s in a steep turn, but as Blue 3 could not drop his tank, he broke away. I carried on and finally

No 91 Sqn pilots gather on and around Sqn Ldr Bond's Spitfire LF IX (NH356) at Manston in early 1945. Issued new to No 91 Sqn on 30 August 1944, LF IX NH356 was duly passed on to No 1 Sqn and written off on 19 April 1945
(Penelope Maskill-Bourke)

out-turned the last ME109, making an attack from ten degrees off at 300 yards' range, closing down to 200, firing a three-second burst. I saw strikes all along the port side of the fuselage and on both wings, after which he flicked over on his back and disappeared into cloud with black smoke pouring out of the aircraft. I did not follow him as the other ME109 and FW190 were getting on to my tail, and since I could not out-turn them I climbed away into sun. I stayed at 2000 ft for a while, where I could see several aircraft being engaged and saw one enemy aircraft go down in flames. I turned for base after this, but as my engine failed and I force-landed at B.79.

'"I claim one ME109 damaged."'

The Armament Report for this mission read as follows:

Pilot	Flt Lt Marshall	Flg Off Faulkner	Flt Lt Topham
Squadron	91	91	91
Section	Yellow 1	Yellow 2	Blue 4
Machine Gun	540	560	500
Cannon	204	96	Approx. 60
Length of film	Not switched on	4 ft	Nil
Claim	2 Bf 109 dest.	1 Bf 109 dest.	1 Bf109 dam.

It had been a great day for the squadron, marred only by the loss of Australian Ken Collier, flying Spitfire MK587. One of the unit's great characters, he was always at the centre of the fun. Collier's place in history, however, was assured when he became the first pilot to 'tip' a 'Diver' in June 1944 – he went on to claim seven V1s destroyed.

The arrival of No 1 Sqn at Manston on 18 December allowed a Spitfire wing to be formed, with Wg Cdr Oxspring as its leader. The Manston Wing soon became a very effective unit, and in the run up to Christmas 1944, it continued to be heavily committed to bomber escort work.

The year ended with some excellent news for the pilots of No 91 Sqn when they learned that they would be the first to receive the latest Spitfire to reach the frontline, the F 21 (Roman numerals were officially used up to XX). This variant would be the fastest of the wartime Spitfires, capable of speeds of up to 454 mph at 26,000 ft, but the major improvement was that its standard armament was four 20 mm Hispano Mk II cannons.

The CO and Flt Lt Huntley had their first flights in an early-production aircraft on New Year's Eve, and the first two F 21s assigned to No 91 Sqn – LA210 and LA212 – were delivered on 4 January 1945. As further aircraft arrived, so the squadron found itself busy with practice flights and cannon tests. The pilots were delighted with the new Supermarine fighter, the only sadness being the fact that they were not permitted to fly them on operations over enemy territory.

As the unit transitioned onto the F 21s, the first operations of the new year were flown in the veteran Spitfire IXs. And with the bombers probing deeper and deeper into Germany, it became necessary to extend the range of the Merlin-engined fighter. For Nos 1 and No 91 Sqns, this was achieved through the use of Advanced Landing Grounds (ALGs) on the

The Manston Wing (Spitfire LF IX-equipped Nos 1 and 91 Sqns) fly in formation over their Kentish base in 1945 (Sqn Ldr Nash)

continent. These were hastily-constructed airfields which were always primitive and usually very damp! No 91 Sqn's 'foreign excursions' began on 5 January when its pilots landed at Ursel (ALG B.67), east of Bruges, following operations – the unit stayed the night, before returning to Manston the following morning.

Despite a lack of enemy air activity, No 91 Sqn was kept busy throughout January, February and March flying Ramrods from Ursel and Maldeghem (ALG B.65). On 28 February it flew Ramrod 1475, escorting 240 Lancasters bombing targets in the Ruhr. No enemy aircraft were seen, but shortly after take-off Flt Lt Draper, flying Spitfire IX ML341, force-landed with engine trouble. Crashing at speed in a field near Maldeghem, he ploughed through a hedge, ripped the wings off the fighter and finally came to rest upside down. Fortunately, he was not seriously injured, but the aircraft was written off.

On 1 March Sqn Ldr I P J 'Mick' Maskill DFC was posted in to command the squadron, the veteran New Zealander having most recently served as a flight commander with No 1 Sqn at Manston.

Eight days after Maskill took command, No 91 Sqn participated in Ramrod 1487 from Maldeghem, escorting Lancasters sent to bomb the Dortmund-Ems canal. Flg Off A G Hyde, flying Spitfire IX MJ623, and acting as R/T relay, asked Manston control for a homing, and then nothing further was heard from him. The mystery was only partially solved the following day when the squadron learned that he had crash-landed at Rennes, in Brittany. This was on the other side of France, and no one could tell why he was so far off course.

Originally captioned 'The Ludham Communists', this photograph does, in fact, show the armourers of No 91 Sqn 'in the field' at Ludham in 1945! The Fordson Standard tractor was used to tow the ammunition trailer (signified by the red flag) out to the dispersals – the men are sitting on boxes of 20 mm ammunition (*Roy Stevens*)

'Spike' Hyde had suffered serious facial injuries and fractured both his spine and skull during the crash, and the squadron was told that he was unlikely to live, despite the best efforts of the 4389th US Military Hospital at Rennes – Flg Off Hyde did, however, survive.

ANTI-SUBMARINE SORTIES & 'JIM CROWS'

On 4 April the squadron was surprised to find that it was being redeployed to Ludham, in Norfolk. Despite exhaustive enquiries, no one could find out the reason for the move, but eventually it was revealed that No 91 Sqn was to be tasked with performing anti-V2 rocket sweeps over Holland, anti-midget submarine patrols and 'Jim Crows'. With the last V2 having been launched against the UK on 27 March, this mission quickly became redundant, but squadron pilots were given ample opportunity to exhibit their finely-honed anti-shipping and 'Jim Crow' skills!

Flt Lt Jimmy Monihan and his Spitfire F 21 at Duxford in 1946. Monihan served with No 91 Sqn from July 1943 until May 1946, when he was demobbed at the Cambridgeshire fighter base. When he enquired as to why he had served so long on the squadron, it was suggested that it was because he was the squadron pianist!
(J Monihan)

On 10 April No 91 Sqn carried out its first Spitfire F 21 operations, early recces over the North Sea discovering two German minesweepers moving north and six barges moving south. Four aircraft were sent to attack them, but were later recalled to Ludham.

During the flight home Flt Lt Cruickshank, flying Spitfire LA234, and Flg Off Faulkner, in Spitfire LA229, attacked shipping off the Dutch port of Den Helder. Encountering particularly accurate defensive fire, both pilots were swiftly shot down into the North Sea. An ASR search found them in their dinghies about eight miles off the Dutch coast, and a Catalina, escorted by four Thunderbolts, went to rescue them.

An airborne lifeboat was also dropped to the men by a Coastal Command Warwick (a version of the Vickers Wellington), but eventually it was the Catalina which picked them up and flew them straight to a US military hospital at Halesworth, in Suffolk. The pilots were not seriously injured, however, and returned to the squadron the next day. At the conclusion of the first Spitfire F 21 operations, AOC No 12 Group visited Ludham to find out how the day had progressed. 'Not particularly well' would have been the honest answer!

With almost no enemy air activity, the squadron found itself busy flying anti-midget submarine patrols and, on 13 April 24 such sorties were flown. At 1205 hrs on 26 April, Flt Lt Draper spotted a midget submarine of the *Biber* class just as it was leaving the Hook of Holland. The attack was described in the following report, which was submitted to HQ No 12 Group:

'Ai/160 Secret Report On Midget Sub Attack 26 April 1945

'Red Section No 91 Sqn, two Spitfire XXIs flown by Flt Lt W C Marshall and Flt Lt J W P Draper DFC (Canadian), were airborne at 1035 hrs on 26 April 1945 on an anti-midget submarine patrol which they

This anonymous aircraft was amongst the first batch of Spitfire F 21s issued to No 91 Sqn in January 1945. It was photographed at Ludham in May 1945 (*via Andy Thomas*)

carried out uneventfully from 1100 to 1200 hrs. Having flown the last leg down to the Schelde, Red 1 decided to return to base from the Hague. While flying northwards to that point Red 2 (Flt Lt Draper) sighted a midget submarine of the *Biber* type heading out to sea just off the mole at the Hook. Red 2 informed Red 1 by R/T and turned 180 degrees to attack, followed by Red 1. Time 1205 hrs.

'The Midget sub was then some 250/300 yards off shore and, despite moderate, but accurate light flak from gun positions on the mole, the section attacked with cannon in dives from 1000 ft down to 50 ft, obtaining strikes on the superstructure around the conning tower, which brought the sub almost to a standstill. The section made a second attack this time in a northerly direction from the same height. Strikes were again scored, and as a result of this second attack the sub was seen to sink, leaving some wreckage and a large patch of oil on the surface. Both pilots fired a short burst at the oil patch and then set course for base, landing at 1230 hrs, claiming the midget submarine as destroyed. Another section of No 91 Sqn subsequently sighted a Red Cross lifeboat searching the vicinity of the attack, obviously looking for survivors.'

Returning to Ludham, the jubilant pilots 'beat up the drome' at very low level, but unfortunately the Sector Group Captain was visiting at the time, and he was not at all impressed. He was not smiling when he said

Cpl Roy Stevens (right) and a fellow armourer work on the 20 mm Hispano cannons of a No 91 Sqn Spitfire F 21 at Ludham in 1945 *(R Stevens)*

No 91 Sqn's VE-Day photograph, taken at Ludham on 10 May 1945. These men are, from left to right (back row), unknown, Len King, unknown, Freddie Lewis, unknown, Charlie Freeman, unknown, Jimmy Monihan, George Balcombe, Alex Smith, 'Doc', Hugh Neil and the squadron Engineering Officer. Front row, left to right, Johnny Faulkner, 'Shag' O'Shaughnessy, 'Mick' Maskill (OC), Geoff Kay and 'Bundu' Baker *(F A Lewis)*

'those two are in for a surprise when they land!' However, when he learned the reason for their antics, the admonishment for unauthorised low flying was forgotten, and it was congratulations all round.

On 1 May the squadron carried out their 152nd sortie from Ludham – another anti-midget submarine patrol, which was aborted due to the weather. It proved to be the unit's last wartime operation, for on 4 May the German armies in the Netherlands, north-west Germany and Denmark surrendered to 21st Army Group Commander, Gen Bernard Montgomery. The occasion was celebrated, naturally enough, with a party at the Sutton Staithe in honour of the Dutchman, Flt Lt Van Eendenberg, who flew over his home town at very low level the very next day.

8 May was proclaimed as VE-Day, with the Great Ludham Victory Dance being held on the 9th. For 48 hours there was no flying for No 91 Sqn, and amid the parties, on the 10th, a squadron photograph was taken as the unit began trying to adjust to RAF peacetime procedure – something most of its personnel had never known before.

In the post-war air force weekend leave was granted, attendance at games' afternoons was strongly encouraged and the wearing of regulation uniform was also enforced! Flying consisted in the main of cross-country flights, exercises and aerobatics.

On 11 May famous Spitfire test pilot Alex Henshaw visited Ludham and put on a superb display of aerobatics (almost certainly in a new Spitfire F 22, which differed from the F 21 in having a cut down rear fuse-lage and a bubble canopy). There was, however, a note of caution from No 91 Sqn's CO, Sqn Ldr Maskill, following the performance. He told all of his pilots that Henshaw had been 'born in a Spitfire', and that under no circumstances were they to attempt to imitate any part of his display.

Spitfire F 21 LA200 is seen at Ludham in the early spring of 1945. Flg Off Geoff Kay was killed whilst practising aerobatics in this aircraft over his Norfolk base on 12 May 1945 *(via E B Morgan)*

Spitfire F 21 LA223 is seen outside the Vickers-Armstrongs factory at Southampton's Hamble Airport in early 1946. This aircraft subsequently served with No 600 Sqn at Biggin Hill until April 1950, when it was withdrawn from use (*via A Thomas*)

Sadly, the next morning at 1100 hrs, Flg Off Geoffrey Kay, flying Spitfire LA200, died when his fighter struck the ground at Ludham whilst practising aerobatics. Unbelievably, 48 hours later Flt Lt Arthur Elcock, in LA203, was killed when he crashed on landing just 100 yards away from where Geoff Kay's accident had taken place. 'Big' Elcock was another squadron stalwart, and a 'Diver' ace, with seven and one shared kills.

THE END

Geoff Kay and 'Big' Elcock were No 91 Sqn's last casualties, and the unit settled into leading the life of a post-war fighter outfit. On 14 July the squadron went to No 18 Armament Practice Camp (APC) at Fairwood

Common, in South Wales, for a month of air-to-air, air-to-ground and cine gun sorties. At the end of the course its pilots deployed to Dyce, near Aberdeen, where they began a series of ASR and interception exercises.

On 21 March 1946 No 91 Sqn finally settled at their permanent peacetime base of Duxford, in Cambridgeshire. Part of the following summer was spent at No 3 Armament Practice School at Lübeck, in Germany, where the unit achieved excellent results, before returning to Duxford to be greeted with the news that it was going to be one of the first squadrons to receive the Meteor III fighter. However, these early jets were extremely unreliable, and No 91 Sqn had just gone operational with them when it was disbanded on 31 January 1947 by being re-numbered No 92 Sqn.

No 91 Sqn's Spitfire F 21s are seen lined up during a post-war victory parade staged during the summer of 1945. Precisely where this event took place remains unclear *(Sqn Ldr Nash)*

In this photograph (taken at the same time as the shot above) No 91 Sqn's large French contingent march past the saluting officer, with Spitfire F 21 LA235/'DL-T' visible in the background *(Sqn Ldr Nash)*

APPENDICES

APPENDIX 1

OFFICERS COMMANDING No 91 SQN

Flt Lt C P Green	8/10/40 (No 421 Flt)	Sqn Ldr N A Kynaston DFC and Bar	19/8/43
Sqn Ldr F C Hopcroft	16/1/41	Sqn Ldr P M Bond	18/8/44
Sqn Ldr C P Green DFC	18/1/41	Sqn Ldr I P J Maskill DFC	1/3/45
Sqn Ldr J N Watts Farmer DFC	11/6/41	Sqn Ldr D E Proudlove	18/1/46
Sqn Ldr H D Cooke	5/9/41	Sqn Ldr A R Hall DFC	19/3/46
Sqn Ldr R W Oxspring DFC and Bar	28/12/41	Sqn Ldr C K Gray DFC	3/4/46
Sqn Ldr J E F Demozay DSO, DFC & Bar	11/7/42	Sqn Ldr E W Wright DFC, DFM	26/10/46
Sqn Ldr R H Harries DSO and Bar, DFC and Bar	8/12/42	Squadron disbanded 31/1/47	

APPENDIX 2

No 91 SQN BASES

Gravesend	8/10/40 (No 421 Flt)	Deanland	21/7/44
West Malling	31/10/40	Biggin Hill	17/10/44
Biggin Hill	6/11/40	Manston	29/10/44
Hawkinge	15/11/40 (No 91 Sqn formed 11/1/41)	Ludham	8/4/45
Lympne	23/11/42	Fairwood Common	14/7/45
Hawkinge	11/1/43	Dyce	18/8/45
Honiley	20/4/43	Duxford	21/3/46
Wittering	9/5/43	West Malling	4/6/46
Kingscliffe	10/5/43	Duxford	10/6/46
Hawkinge	21/5/43	Lubeck	29/6/46
Westhampnett	28/6/43	Duxford	30/8/46
Tangmere	4/10/43	Acklington	6/1/47
Castle Camps	29/2/44		
Drem	8/3/44		
West Malling	23/4/44	Squadron disbanded 31/1/47 (re-numbered as No 92 Sqn)	

APPENDIX 3

AIRCRAFT USED BY No 91 SQN

Spitfire IIA

Wing Span: 36 ft 10 in
Engine: Rolls-Royce Merlin XII (1150 hp)
Maximum Speed: 357 mph at 17,000 ft
Ceiling: 37,600 ft
Armament: 8 x 0.303-in Browning machine guns
The Spitfire IIA was used by No 421 Flt from its formation on 8 October 1940 until 12 October, when ten Hurricane IIAs arrived. On 6 November the flight was re-equipped once again with Spitfire IIAs. These were retained until 4 May 1941, when Spitfire VBs were issued in their place.

Hurricane IIA

Wing Span: 40 ft 0 in
Engine: Rolls-Royce Merlin XX (1280 hp)
Maximum Speed: 342 mph at 22,000 ft
Ceiling: 36,300 ft
Armament: 8 x 0.303-in Browning machine guns
No 421 Flt was the first unit to be issued with the Hurricane IIA, but used them only briefly from 12 October to 6 November 1940.

Spitfire VB/VC

Wing Span: 36 ft 10 in (LF VB, 32 ft 2 in)
Engine: Rolls-Royce Merlin 45 (1440 hp)
Maximum Speed: 374 mph at 13,000 ft (LF VB, 357 at 6000 ft)
Ceiling: 37,000 ft (LF VB, 36,500 ft)
Armament: VB had 2 x 20 mm Hispano cannons and 4 x 0.303-in Browning machine guns; VC as above, or 4 x 20 mm Hispano cannons
No 91 Sqn was the second unit to receive the Spitfire VB, re-equipping on 4 May 1941. The squadron also used some LF VBs from late 1941 onwards, this version having been optimised for low altitude operations by having its wings clipped and engine modified. No 91 Sqn also used at least three Spitfire VCs. The squadron retained the VBs until May 1943, when they were superseded by the Spitfire F XII.

Spitfire VI

Wing Span: 40 ft 2 in
Engine: Rolls-Royce Merlin 47 (1415 hp)
Maximum Speed: 364 mph at 21,500 ft
Ceiling: 40,000 ft
Armament: 2 x 20 mm Hispano cannons and 4 x 0.303-in Browning machine guns
Only 100 examples of the Spitfire VI were produced, and No 91 Sqn was one of the earliest units to be issued with the high-altitude fighter. The squadron received seven Mk VIs, the first being AB498 (the fourth production aircraft) on 22 June 1942. No 91 Sqn did not keep the Mk VI for long,

however, and they had all been reissued to other squadrons by 18 September 1942.

Spitfire F XII

Wing Span: 32 ft 7 in
Engine: Rolls-Royce Griffon III/IV (1735 hp)
Maximum Speed: 393 mph at 18,000 ft
Ceiling: 40,000 ft
Armament: 2 x 20 mm Hispano cannons and 4 x 0.303-in Browning machine guns
The first of the Griffon-engined Spitfires, the Spitfire F XII was only issued to two squadrons, with No 91 Sqn being the second unit to receive them. It continued to use them to good effect until the F XIV arrived in March 1944.

Spitfire F XIV

Wing Span: 36 ft 10 in
Engine: Rolls-Royce Griffon 65 (2050 hp)
Maximum Speed: 448 mph at 26,000 ft
Ceiling: 44,500 ft
Armament: 2 x 20 mm Hispano cannons and 4 x 0.303-in Browning machine guns
No 91 Sqn was the second squadron to be equipped with the Spitfire F XIV, receiving them in March 1944. This variant was used to good effect throughout the 'Diver' campaign, and then exchanged for Spitfire LF IXs on 9 August 1944.

Spitfire LF IX

Wing Span: 32 ft 2 in
Engine: Rolls-Royce Merlin 66 (1720 hp)
Maximum Speed: 404 mph at 21,000 ft
Ceiling: 42,500 ft
Armament: 2 x 20 mm Hispano cannons and 4 x 0.303-in Browning machine guns
No 91 Sqn inherited most of its Spitfire LF IXs from No 402 'Canadian' Sqn, and retained them until early 1945, when the F 21s arrived.

Spitfire F 21

Wing Span: 36 ft 11 in
Engine: Rolls-Royce Griffon 61 (2050 hp)
Maximum Speed: 454 mph at 26,000 ft
Ceiling: 43,500 ft
Armament: 4 x 20 mm Hispano Mk II cannons
No 91 Sqn was the first unit to receive the Spitfire F 21. The first aircraft arrived on 4 January 1945, and the squadron continued to operate them until completing a lengthy conversion onto the Meteor 3 in October 1946. The last Spitfire F 21s were returned to Maintenance Units on 11 October 1946.

APPENDIX 4

No 91 SQN ROLL OF HONOUR

11/10/40

Sgt Charles Albert Henry Ayling. Shot down in Spitfire IIA P7303 by Bf 109s, crashing at Newchurch, Kent. He was buried in Monkton St Nicholas Cemetery, Pembroke.

31/12/40

Sgt Maurice Alexander William Lee. Killed trying to land at Biggin Hill in bad weather in Spitfire IIA coded 'LZ-F'. He was buried in St Mary Cray Cemetery, Orpington, Kent.

10/2/41

Flg Off Peter McDonnell Hartas. Flew into a hill south-east of Hawkinge in low cloud in Spitfire IIA P7888. He was buried at Hawkinge, Kent.

26/4/41

Flt Sgt Andrew Smitton Darling. Shot down by Bf 109s in Spitfire IIA, P7615, crashing in Reindene Wood, near Hawkinge. He was buried in Auchterader, Perthshire.

16/6/41

Plt Off Douglas Hugh Gage. Failed to return from ASR escort in Spitfire VB W3126. He is commemorated on Panel 32 of the Runnymede Memorial.

1/7/41

Sgt Frederick Aaron Thornber. Failed to return from shipping recce to Le Touquet in Spitfire VB R7340, and his body was recovered from the sea on 5 July. He was buried in Hawkinge, Kent.

9/9/41

Sgt James Enerton Cooper. Failed to return from ASR practice off Dungeness in a Spitfire VB (serial not known). He was buried in Luton General Cemetery, Bedfordshire.

1/10/41

Plt Off Noel Proctor Warden. Shot down by Bf 109s in a Spitfire VB (possibly R7290) whilst escorting an HSL. He is commemorated on Panel 35 of the Runnymede Memorial.

1/10/41

Sgt Gerald William Baker. Shot down by Bf 109s in a Spitfire VB (possibly R7290) whilst escorting an HSL. He was buried in The Hague (West Duin) Cemetery, The Netherlands.

17/11/41

Plt Off Archibald William Black. Failed to return from shipping recce to the Somme area in Spitfire VB coded 'DL-W' (serial not recorded). He is commemorated on Panel 31 of the Runnymede Memorial.

8/2/42

Flt Lt John Denys Fletcher. Failed to return from shipping recce to Ostend in Spitfire VB W3132. He was buried in Middelkerke, Belgium.

15/6/42

Sgt Edwin Edward Sykes. Failed to return from Dieppe recce in Spitfire VB AR370. He is commemorated on Panel 107 of the Runnymede Memorial.

15/7/42

Flt Sgt Frederick Yorston Campbell. Shot down by Fw 190s off Hastings in Spitfire VB, BL662. He is commemorated on Panel 102 of the Runnymede Memorial.

22/7/42

Flt Lt William Boyd Orr. Failed to return from Dieppe recce in Spitfire VB BL816. He is commemorated on Panel 66 of the Runnymede Memorial.

4/8/42

Plt Off Raymond Kenneth James Wildish. Failed to return from patrol in poor weather in Spitfire VB BL683. He is commemorated on Panel 72 of the Runnymede Memorial.

20/8/42

Plt Off Edwyn Tonge. Failed to return from post-Dieppe landing operation in Spitfire VB BM558. He is commemorated on Panel 72 of the Runnymede Memorial.

27/8/42

Plt Off Henry Jean Marc de Molenes. Killed bailing out of fuel-starved Spitfire VB BL230 whilst on ASR escort. He was initially buried at Hawkinge, but his body was repatriated to France post-war.

11/9/42

Flt Lt Arthur Gerald Donahue DFC. Missing from Ostend recce in Spitfire VB BL511, having claimed a probably destroyed Ju 88 off the French or Belgian coast. He is commemorated on Panel 65 of the Runnymede Memorial.

23/9/42

Plt Off John Baxter Edwards. Missing from Ostend recce in Spitfire VB EN844. He is commemorated on Panel 69 of the Runnymede Memorial.

31/10/42

Flg Off Ronald Gordon Vicary Gibbs. Failed to return from combat with Fw 190s over Canterbury in Spitfire VB AD458. He is commemorated on Panel 67 of the Runnymede Memorial.

2/11/42
Flt Lt Alan Jeffrey Andrews DFC and Bar. Missing from shipping recce/ASR search from Boulogne to Dieppe in Spitfire VB AB378. He is commemorated on Panel 65 of the Runnymede Memorial.

6/12/42
Flg Off Gordon Harry Dean. Missing from Dieppe recce in a Spitfire VB (either AB982 or BL536). He is commemorated on Panel 66 of the Runnymede Memorial.

6/12/42
Plt Off Melville Kerson Eldrid. Missing from Dieppe recce in a Spitfire VB (either AB982 or BL536). He is commemorated on Panel 69 of the Runnymede Memorial.

7/12/42
Plt Off J P Coudray. Missing from Ostend recce in Spitfire VB BL853. Place of burial/commemoration unknown. Many Free French pilots used aliases to protect families at home. It is believed that J P Coudray was the *nom de guerre* of J P Lux.

18/12/42
Sgt Jack Charles Chittick. Shot down in error by Typhoons of No 609 Sqn whilst flying Spitfire VB EP508. He is commemorated on Panel 80 of the Runnymede Memorial.

29/12/42
Plt Off Irwin William Downer. Shot down by an Fw 190 during Dungeness to Beachy Head patrol in Spitfire VB EN782. He is commemorated on Panel 115 of the Runnymede Memorial.

8/3/43
Flg Off James Gilbert Johnson. Missing from Ostend recce in Spitfire VB AB894. He is commemorated on Panel 188 of the Runnymede Memorial.

24/3/43
Flg Off Raymond Gustave Hector de Hasse. Shot down by Fw 190s off Dungeness in Spitfire VB W3425. He is commemorated on Panel 124 of the Runnymede Memorial.

16/6/43
Sgt Willie Mitchell. Missing from ASR operations south-east of Dover in Spitfire XII MB835. He is commemorated on Panel 159 of the Runnymede Memorial.

19/9/43
Flg Off Geoffrey William Bond. Failed to return from Ramrod 232 in Spitfire XII EN614. He was buried at Coxyde Military Cemetery, Belgium.

24/9/43
Flt Lt Gray Stenborg DFC. Failed to return from Ramrod 241 in Spitfire XII MB805. He was buried at Marissel French National cemetery, France

6/12/43
Flg Off Frederick Dash Thomas. Collided with Flg Off H F Heninger whilst flying Spitfire XII EN604 during formation flying practice and crashed near East Grinstead. He was buried in St James' churchyard, Stivichall, Warwickshire.

6/1/44
Flg Off Harold Frederick Heninger. Missing from bomber escort operation in Rouen area in Spitfire XII EN223. He was buried at Grandcourt War Cemetery, France.

23/1/44
Flg Off Cameron Livingston McNeil. Crashed during bombing practice at Pagham Harbour in Spitfire XII EN624. He was buried in Brookwood Military Cemetery, Surrey.

31/1/44
Flg Off Derek Roland Inskip. Collided with Flt Sgt R K Fairbairn whilst flying Spitfire XII EN613 on Ramrod 500. He is commemorated on Panel 207 of the Runnymede Memorial.

31/1/44
Flt Sgt Robert Kerr Yule Fairbairn. Collided with Flg Off D R Inskip whilst flying Spitfire XII EN618 on Ramrod 500. He is commemorated on Panel 217 of the Runnymede Memorial.

12/3/44
Flt Sgt Charles Edward Sayer. Failed to return from scramble and crashed south of Edinburgh in Spitfire XIV RB172. He was buried in St Thomas' (Exwick) Cemetery, Exeter.

29/4/44
Flg Off John Arundel Collis. Failed to return from night patrol over Thames estuary in Spitfire XIV RB187. He is commemorated on Panel 205 of the Runnymede Memorial.

25/6/44
Wt Off Richmond Antony Barrett Blumer. Failed to return from 'Diver' patrol and crashed near Nettlestead, Kent in Spitfire XIV RM617. He was buried in Brookwood Military Cemetery, Surrey.

26/7/44
Flt Lt Eugene Georges Achilles Seghers DFC. Collided with V1 over Uckfield and crashed in Spitfire XIV RM743 near East Hoathley, Sussex. He was initially buried in the UK, but his body was repatriated to Belgium post-war.

31/7/44
Flg Off Patrick Alfred Schade DFM. Collided with No 486 Sqn Tempest V flown by Plt Off A A Wilson and crashed north of Bexhill in Spitfire XIV RM654. He was buried in Uxbridge.

3/8/44
Flt Lt Jean Pierre Edmond Maridor DFC. Spitfire XIV RM656 damaged by explosion of V1 and crashed at Benenden, Kent.

He was initially buried in Brookwood Military Cemetery, Surrey, but his body was repatriated to Ste Marie Cemetery, Le Havre, in France, post-war.

15/8/44

Sqn Ldr Norman Arthur Kynaston DFC and Bar. Spitfire IX MK909 hit by flak whilst on Rodeo 381 and he bailed out into the Channel but was not found. He is commemorated on Panel 200 of the Runnymede Memorial.

28/10/44

Sqn Ldr George St Clair Boyd Reid. Failed to return from Ramrod 1349 in Spitfire IX MK453. He was initially given a burial in Slijpe, near Ostend, Belgium, but in 1996 his body was recovered from the cockpit of his aircraft in Maldegem, west of Bruges, Belgium. He was buried at the Canadian Military Cemetery in Adegem, his original 'grave' being re-marked as that of an unknown airman.

5/12/44

Flg Off Kenneth Roy Collier. Failed to return from Ramrod 1394 in Spitfire IX MK587. He was buried at Rheinberg War Cemetery, Germany.

12/5/45

Flg Off Geoffrey Kay. Crashed whilst practising aerobatics at Ludham in Spitfire F 21 LA200. He was buried in Abbey Lane cemetery, Sheffield.

14/5/45

Flt Lt Arthur Richard Elcock. Crashed on landing at Ludham in Spitfire F 21 LA203. He was buried in Smethwick Upland cemetery, Warley, Staffordshire.

APPENDIX 5

DECORATIONS AWARDED TO PILOTS OF No 91 SQN

This appendix entry lists the decorations that were awarded to pilots during their time with No 91 Sqn. The dates shown are those on which the squadron was notified of the award, and not necessarily when it was initially authorised or actually presented to the recipient. The decorations listed are the Distinguished Service Order (DSO), the Distinguished Flying Cross (DFC) and the Distinguished Flying Medal (DFM).

Date	Decoration	Recipient
20/12/40	DFC	Flt Lt B Drake
20/12/40	DFM	Sgt D A S McKay
5/3/41	Bar to DFC	Flg Off J J O'Meara DFC
8/3/41	Bar to DFM	Sgt D A S McKay DFM
5/4/41	DFC	Sqn Ldr C P Green
12/4/41	DFM	Sgt J Mann
15/5/41	DFM	Sgt J Gillies
4/10/41	DFC	Flt Lt J J Le Roux
21/6/42	DFC	Flg Off A J Andrews
21/6/42	DFC	Flt Lt G C R Pannell
30/6/42	Bar to DFC	Sqn Ldr J E F Demozay
2/8/42	DFC	Flt Lt R L Spurdle
2/8/42	DFM	Flt Sgt D J Prytherch
13/11/42	Bar to DFC	Flt Lt A J Andrews DFC (posthumous award)
13/11/42	DFC	Flt Lt R M D Hall
25/11/42	DFC	Flg Off J P E Maridor
2/12/42	DSO	Sqn Ldr J E F Demozay DFC & Bar
16/5/43	Bar to DFC	Sqn Ldr R H Harries DFC
24/7/43	DFC	Flt Lt I G S Matthew
24/9/43	DFC	Flg Off J A Round
16/10/43	DFC	Flt Lt J C S Doll
23/10/43	DFC	Sqn Ldr N A Kynaston
9/5/44	DFC	Flg Off J Andrieux
9/44	Bar to DFC	Sqn Ldr N A Kynaston DFC (posthumous award)
19/9/44	DFC	Flt Lt R S Nash
15/4/45	DFC	Sqn Ldr I P J Maskill
8/45	DFC	Flt Lt W C Marshall
19/10/45	DFC	Flt Lt H D Johnson

Totals:	DSO – 1
	DFC – 22 (including five Bars)
	DFM – 5 (including one Bar)

APPENDIX 6

No 91 SQN ACES

Many of the RAF's best fighter pilots spent time on No 91 Sqn. Some were at the very beginning of their careers, whilst others achieved five or more aerial victories flying with the squadron, and thus became aces. A few, however, came to the unit with a considerable number of claims already (including Malta aces 'Paddy' Schade and Gray Stenborg). The pilots shown in this appendix each claimed five or more aerial victories, and at some time served on No 91 Sqn. The decorations shown are those awarded either prior to, or during, their service with No 91 Sqn, and the ranks shown are those held on leaving the unit.

Flg Off Jacques Andrieux DFC

'Jaco' Andrieux (6 destroyed, 4 probables and 2 damaged) joined No 91 Sqn on 6 July 1943 and left on 17 June 1944 when he was posted to No 341 'French' Sqn. During his time with No 91 Sqn he made five claims.

Flg Off Henry Collingham Baker

Henry Baker (5 and 2 shared destroyed, 1 probable and 6 damaged) was posted to No 421 Flt as one of its original pilots on 8 October 1940. He joined No 306 'Polish' Sqn on 12 December 1940, having made six claims.

Flg Off Patrick Peter Colum Barthropp

'Paddy' Barthropp (2 and 2 shared destroyed, 1 probable and 3 damaged) joined No 91 Sqn on 5 February 1941, and went on to make five claims before being posted to No 610 Sqn on 24 August that same year.

Sqn Ldr Jean-Francois Demozay DSO, DFC and Bar

Jean Demozay (18 destroyed, 2 probables, 4 damaged, 1 destroyed on the ground, 1 probable on the ground and 3 damaged on the ground) was posted to No 91 Sqn on 1 July 1941. His tally of claims rose quickly whilst with the unit, and he was soon promoted, being posted to HQ No 11 Group on 1 February 1942. His second tour on No 91 Sqn began on 11 July that same year, when he was posted in as CO. Demozay made several more claims before finally leaving the squadron on 8 December 1942. His total of claims made whilst serving with No 91 Sqn was 23, easily making him the squadron's highest-scoring pilot.

Flt Lt John Christopher Shaboe Doll DFC

'Chris' Doll (4 destroyed, 1 shared destroyed and 1 damaged) joined No 91 Sqn on 1 September 1943, making five claims up to 26 April 1944, when he was wounded and left the unit.

Flt Lt Arthur Gerald Donahue DFC

'Art' Donahue (2 destroyed, 2 probables and 1 damaged) was posted to No 91 Sqn on 20 February 1941, and all of his claims were made whilst with the unit. On 29 October that same year, he was posted to No 258 Sqn in the Far East, but returned to No 91 Sqn on 20 August 1942 as 'A' Flight commander. He was posted 'Missing' on 11 September, following combat with a Ju 88 off the Dutch or Belgian coast.

Flt Lt B Drake DFC

Billy Drake (20 and 2 shared destroyed, 2 unconfirmed destroyed, 4 and 2 shared probables, 7 damaged, 13 destroyed on the ground and 4 damaged on the ground) joined No 421 Flt in October 1940. When it became No 91 Sqn in January 1941, Drake was given command of 'A' Flight. He remained in the post until he left the squadron on 11 February, having made five claims.

Flt Lt John William Petterson Draper DFC

John Draper (4 and 1 shared destroyed, 2 probables, 1 damaged and 6 V1s destroyed) joined No 91 Sqn on 14 June 1944 and served until June 1945, when he returned home to Canada. He made no claims whilst with No 91 Sqn, apart from his V1 kills.

Flt Sgt James Gillies DFM

'Jim' Gillies (5 and 1 shared destroyed, 1 and 1 shared probable and 2 shared destroyed) was posted to No 421 Flt on 8 October 1940 as one of its original pilots, and he remained with No 91 Sqn until 13 November 1941, having made four claims during his tour.

Sqn Ldr Charles Patrick Green DFC

'Paddy' Green (11 destroyed, 3 and 1 shared probables and 1 damaged) was the first Commanding Officer of No 421 Flt. He made three claims at this time, before becoming the first CO of No 91 Sqn, remaining in the post until 11 June 1941.

Sqn Ldr Raymond Hiley Harries DFC and Bar

'Ray' Harries (15 and 3 shared destroyed, 2 probables, 5 and 1 shared damaged and 1 V1 destroyed) was posted to No 91 Sqn as its CO on 8 December 1942. He left to command the Tangmere Wing on 19 August 1943, having made 12 claims whilst with No 91 Sqn.

Flt Lt Robert Hugh Holland DFC

'Bob' Holland (5 and 1 shared destroyed, 2 and 2 shared

121

unconfirmed destroyed, 4 probables and 6 and 1 shared damaged) was posted to No 91 Sqn as 'A' Flight commander on 13 February 1941. He was posted away for a rest in November, having made three claims.

Sqn Ldr Norman Arthur Kynaston DFC and Bar

Norman Kynaston (4 and 1 shared destroyed, 1 probable, 1 damaged and 22 V1s destroyed) joined No 91 Sqn on 18 November 1942. All of his claims were made whilst with the squadron, and he went on to become the CO on 19 August 1943. On 15 August 1944 Kynaston was posted 'Missing' from Rodeo 381, when his aircraft was damaged by flak and he was forced to bail out over the sea.

Plt Off Keith Ashley Lawrence

Keith Lawrence (4 and 2 shared destroyed and 9 and 1 shared damaged) was posted to No 421 Flt on 8 October 1940 as one of its original pilots. On 27 November he was shot down by Bf 109s, bailing out into the sea with leg and arm injuries. On his recovery in early 1941 he rejoined No 91 Sqn, and in January 1942 he was posted to No 185 Sqn, having made one claim.

Flt Lt Roland Anthony Lee-Knight

Tony Lee-Knight (5 and 1 shared destroyed, 3 probables, 3 damaged and 1 destroyed on the ground) was posted to No 91 Sqn as 'B' Flight commander in January 1941, and he made his first claims with the unit. On 9 June that same year he was posted to No 610 Sqn, having made four claims.

Flt Lt Johannes Jacobus Le Roux DFC and Bar

'Chris' Le Roux (18 destroyed, 2 probables and 8 damaged) joined No 91 Sqn on 20 February 1941 and immediately began to amass a large number of claims. He left the squadron on 3 December 1941, but returned on 16 September 1942, having carried out instructor duties and work for Rolls-Royce. Le Roux left the unit for the last time on 23 November 1942, having made 13 claims.

Sgt Jack Mann DFM

Jackie Mann (5 destroyed, 1 probable and 3 damaged) joined No 91 Sqn on 5 February 1941, and had a brief but eventful time with the unit, making one claim and being shot down twice in quick succession. He left the squadron, having being wounded for the last time, on 4 April 1941.

Flt Lt Jean Pierre Edmond Maridor DFC

Jean Maridor (3 and 1 shared destroyed, 2 probables, 3 damaged and 5 and 2 shared V1s destroyed) was posted to No 91 Sqn on 14 February 1942. Having made eight claims, he was still serving with the squadron on 3 August 1944 when he destroyed a V1 at very close range and was killed in the explosion.

Sgt Donald Alistair Stewart McKay DFM and Bar

Don McKay (16 and 1 shared destroyed, 3 unconfirmed destroyed and 5 damaged) was posted to No 421 Flt on 22 October 1940. Seeing much action, he made 11 claims and remained with No 91 Sqn until 14 June 1941, when he was finally posted for a rest.

Flg Off James Joseph O'Meara DFC and Bar

'Orange' O'Meara (11 and 2 shared destroyed, 1 unconfirmed destroyed, 4 probables and 11 and 1 shared damaged) joined No 421 Flt on 8 October 1940 as one of its original pilots. He subsequently made seven claims, before leaving No 91 Sqn on 6 April 1941.

Sqn Ldr Robert Wardlow Oxspring DFC

'Bobby' Oxspring (13 and 2 shared destroyed, 2 probables, 12 damaged and 4 and 1 shared V1s destroyed) was posted to command No 91 Sqn on 28 December 1941. He made no claims with the unit, however, and was posted to No 72 Sqn as its CO on 11 July 1942.

Flg Off Patrick Alfred Schade DFM

'Paddy' Schade (13 and 1 shared destroyed, 3 and 1 shared probables, 2 damaged and 3 and 1 shared V1s destroyed) was posted to No 91 Sqn on 9 October 1943. He made no further claims (except his V1 kills), and was still serving with the squadron on 31 July 1944 when his aircraft collided with a No 485 Sqn Tempest near Bexhill, killing both pilots.

Flt Lt Robert Lawrence Spurdle DFC

'Spud' Spurdle (10 destroyed, 2 and 1 shared probables and 9 and 2 shared damaged) joined No 91 Sqn on 15 April 1941, but left soon afterwards, on 23 May, to join the Merchant Ship Fighter Unit. He returned to No 91 Sqn on 20 February 1942, becoming the commander of 'A' Flight on 10 April, and finally left on 27 August 1942, having made seven claims.

Flt Lt Gray Stenborg DFC

Gray Stenborg (14 and 1 shared destroyed and 3 damaged) was posted to No 91 Sqn on 18 May 1943, and he made five claims in the summer of 1943. Stenborg was shot down and killed over Beauvais in a No 91 Sqn Spitfire F XII on 24 September 1943.

Sqn Ldr Eric William Wright DFC, DFM

'Ricky' Wright (3 and 3 shared destroyed, 3 probables and 8 and 1 shared damaged) was the CO of No 91 Sqn from 26 October 1946 until its disbandment on 31 January 1947.

APPENDIX 7

No 91 SQN 'DIVER' ACES

No 91 Sqn ended the 'Diver' campaign having destroyed a total of 189 V1s (officially, this tally was 185). The squadron was the highest-scoring Spitfire unit of the period, and the third-highest overall (beaten by Nos 3 and 486 Sqns, operating Tempest Vs). Sqn Ldr Kynaston and Flt Lt Nash were the 11th and 15th highest-scoring pilots respectively, and there were six No 91 Sqn pilots in the 'top ten' of highest-scoring Spitfire pilots. The pilots listed here all destroyed five or more V1s whilst serving on No 91 Sqn.

Sqn Ldr Peter McCall Bond – 7 and 3 shared
Flg Off Kenneth Roy Collier – 7
Flg Off A Roy Cruickshank – 10 and 1 shared

Lt Henri F de Bordas – 9 and 1 shared
Flt Lt John William Petterson Draper DFC – 6
Flg Off Arthur Richard Elcock – 7 and 1 shared
Flg Off John A Faulkner – 4 and 2 shared
Flt Lt Herbert Dennis Johnson DFC – 13 and 1 shared
Sqn Ldr Norman Arthur Kynaston DFC and Bar – 22
Flt Lt Jean Pierre Edmond Maridor DFC – 5 and 2 shared
Flg Off William Cyril Marshall – 7
Flg Off R A McPhie – 5 and 3 shared
Flt Lt H Bruce Moffett – 8
Flt Lt Raymond Stanley Nash DFC – 17 and 3 shared
Flg Off Hugh M Neil – 5
Flg Off Edward Topham – 9 and 1 shared

COLOUR PLATES

1

Hurricane IIA Z2345 of Sgt Frederick Perkin, No 421 Flt, Gravesend, October 1940
Frederick Perkin was posted to No 421 Flt from No 73 Sqn on 25 October 1940, and he continued to serve on No 91 Sqn until 28 August 1941, when he was commissioned and posted to No 58 OTU. He briefly returned to No 91 Sqn in the summer of 1942, before being posted to No 111 Sqn. Perkin's association with the 'Nigeria' Squadron continued in 1944, when he served as a fighter controller, based at Hythe, during the 'Diver' campaign. Hurricane IIA Z2345 was one of the first Mk IIs built, and it was issued to No 421 Flt on 12 October 1940. Damaged exactly two weeks later when Sgt Perkin force-landed through high tension cables at South Darenth, it was later repaired and returned to service. Z2345 was eventually sent to the USSR on 8 October 1941. With No 421 Flt being formed on 8 October 1940 as a detached flight of No 66 Sqn, the flight inherited its code letters from the squadron. In order to differentiate between aircraft from the two units, fighters from No 421 Flt had a square dot painted between the code letters.

2

Hurricane IIA Z2352 of Flg Off Dennis Parrott, No 421 Flt, Gravesend, October 1940
Dennis Parrott was posted to No 421 Flt from No 19 Sqn (where he had claimed one Bf 109 destroyed) in October 1940. He served with the unit until 12 December, when he was posted to No 306 'Polish' Sqn. Parrott returned to No 91 Sqn on 11 January 1941, but left soon after and was killed on 22 June 1941 whilst serving with No 29 Sqn – his Beaufighter IF crashed in bad weather near Paddock Wood, Kent, during a routine night sortie. Like Z2345, featured in the previous profile, Hurricane IIA Z2352 was one of the first Mk IIs built, being issued to No 421 Flt on

12 October 1940. The fighter was damaged one week later when Flg Off Parrott force-landed it at Clement Street in Old Swanley. Once repaired, the fighter subsequently saw service with Rolls-Royce as a trials aircraft, followed by No 55 OTU at RAF Usworth. It was Struck off Charge (SoC) on 10 July 1944.

3

Spitfire IIA P7499 of Plt Off Keith Lawrence, No 421 Flt, Hawkinge, November 1940
New Zealander Keith Lawrence (4 and 1 shared destroyed and 9 and 1 shared damaged) joined No 421 Flt as one of its original pilots on 8 October 1940. He remained with the unit until 27 November when, flying P7499, he was shot down off Deal by Bf 109E ace Oberleutnant Gustav 'Mickey' Sprick, Staffelkapitän of 8./JG 26. Lawrence bailed out into the sea and was quickly rescued by a fishing trawler, having been badly wounded. P7499 was delivered new to No 421 Flt on 2 November 1940, and 13 days later Sgt D A S McKay used it to destroy Do 17Z-3 5K+FN of 5./KG 3 off Folkestone.

4

Spitfire IIA P7531 of Flt Lt Charles Green, OC No 421 Flt, Hawkinge, November 1940
Charles 'Paddy' Green (11 destroyed, 3 and 1 shared probable and 1 damaged) was the CO of No 421 Flt, and remained in command after the formation of No 91 Sqn on 11 January 1941. Following its acceptance by the RAF in late October 1940, Spitfire IIA P7531 spent a week with RAE Farnborough on diving trials, prior to being issued to No 421 Flt on 8 November 1940. The fighter continued to serve with No 91 Sqn until it was shot down off Ostend by Unteroffizier Amhausend of I./JG 2 on 24 April 1941. Its pilot, Plt Off Peall, bailed out and was rescued by the Margate lifeboat.

5
Spitfire IIA P7307 of Sgt Donald McKay, No 91 Sqn, Hawkinge, February 1941

Don McKay (16 and 1 shared destroyed, 3 unconfirmed destroyed and 5 damaged) was posted to No 421 Flt on 22 October 1940, and remained with the unit until 14 June 1941, when he was posted for a rest to No 55 OTU. He was flying P7307 on 4 February 1941 when he destroyed a Bf 109E and damaged another off Deal – both fighters were from II./JG 3. Built in July 1940, P7307 was issued to No 421 Flt on 30 December 1940, having already seen action with Nos 266 and 603 Sqns in the Battle of Britain. Passed on to No 65 Sqn in April 1941, the fighter subsequently served with Nos 308 'Polish' and 154 Sqns and No 61 OTU. P7307 was written off in a mid-air collision with Spitfire VB BM140 of No 315 'Polish' Sqn on 15 March 1942 whilst still serving with the OTU.

6
Spitfire IIA P8194 *GOLD COAST I* of Sgt Donald McKay, No 91 Sqn, Hawkinge, April 1941

Issued to No 91 Sqn on 9 April 1941, P8194 subsequently served with Nos 234, 66 and 152 Sqns, in that order. After a spell at No 57 OTU in 1942, the aircraft was used on propeller trials by de Havilland at Boscombe Down, before being written off in an accident on 28 January 1944.

7
Spitfire VB W3122 of Flt Lt Jean Demozay, No 91 Sqn, Hawkinge, July 1941

Jean Demozay (18 destroyed, 2 probables, 4 damaged, 1 destroyed on the ground, 1 probable on the ground and 3 damaged on the ground) joined No 91 Sqn on 1 July 1941, and served until 1 February 1942. Returning as CO on 11 July 1942, he commanded the unit until 8 December 1942. W3122 was issued to No 91 Sqn on 29 April 1941 – ahead of most of the squadron's new Mk VBs. Frequently flown by Demozay, it left the squadron on 8 December 1941 and was converted to LF VB standard by Air Service Training Ltd at its Hamble factory. Reissued to No 111 Sqn on 3 May 1942, the veteran fighter ended its days as an instructional airframe at No 10 School of Technical Training.

8
Spitfire VB W3135 of Sgt John Down, No 91 Sqn, Hawkinge, November 1941

John Down was one of No 91 Sqn's longest serving pilots, being credited with two damaged claims during his spell with the unit. Having briefly flown with Nos 64, 616 and 611 Sqns, he arrived on the 'Nigeria' Squadron in February 1941. Posted to No 52 OTU for a rest on 15 November that same year, Down rejoined No 91 Sqn on 1 August 1942 as a flight sergeant, and was commissioned in September from warrant officer. He finally left the unit on 27 July 1943 as a pilot officer, going to the Air Fighting Development Unit (AFDU). Down briefly flew Spitfire VB W3135 at the end of his first tour, the fighter having been issued to No 91 Sqn from long-term storage with No 8 MU in November 1941. In April 1942 it left the squadron and went to Air Service Training Ltd at Hamble for conversion into an LF VB, and it was subsequently modified into a low-level fighter-recce PR XIII. Issued to No 541 Sqn, W3135 was finally Struck off Charge on 26 February 1945.

9
Spitfire VC AA976 *GRAND HOTEL MANCHESTER* of Flt Lt Frank Silk, No 91 Sqn, Hawkinge, May 1942

Frank Silk joined No 91 Sqn as a sergeant pilot in 1941, but was commissioned in November and went on to command 'B' Flight. He left the squadron on 1 July 1942, being posted to Hawkers as a test pilot. AA976 was one of the Spitfires he flew regularly during the spring of 1942, the fighter arriving new on No 91 Sqn on 14 March. It was fitted with a 'Universal' wing capable of housing either four 20 mm cannons and no machine guns, two 20 mm cannons and four machine guns or eight machine guns. The Mk VCs flown by No 91 Sqn were usually configured as shown here, with two 20 mm cannons and four 0.303-in machine guns, as per the standard Mk VB. AA976 remained with the unit until 9 June 1943, and after being reworked by Vickers Supermarine into an LF VB, it saw service in 1944 with Nos 130, 222 and 322 Sqns. The fighter was finally Struck off Charge on 10 January 1946. AA976 was fitted with both Merlin 45 and 46 engines during its long career.

10
Spitfire VC AB216 *Nigeria OYO PROVINCE* of Sqn Ldr Robert Oxspring, OC No 91 Sqn, Hawkinge, May 1942

'Bobby' Oxspring (13 and 2 shared destroyed, 2 probables, 12 damaged and 4 and 1 shared V1s destroyed) commanded No 91 Sqn from 28 December 1941 through to 11 July 1942, but made no claims whilst with the unit. AB216 was issued new to No 91 Sqn on 15 March 1942, and was damaged on operations on 2 June 1943. Following repairs, it was used by the Aeroplane & Armament Experimental Establishment (A&AEE) in extensive trials towing Hotspur and Horsa gliders in conjunction with other aircraft, including a Beaufighter. The aircraft was written off on 2 February 1945 following a wheels up landing caused by an in-flight engine fire.

11
Spitfire VC AB248 *Nigeria IJUBU PROVINCE* of Flt Lt Robert Spurdle, No 91 Sqn, Lympne, May 1942

Battle of Britain veteran 'Spud' Spurdle (10 destroyed, 2 and 1 shared probables and 9 and 2 shared damaged) initially joined No 91 Sqn from No 74 Sqn on 15 April 1941, but left again on 23 May to join the Merchant Ship Fighter Unit. He returned to the 'Nigeria' Squadron on 20 February 1942, becoming OC 'A' Flight on 10 April – a post he held until he left the unit on 27 August 1942. AB248 was issued new to No 91 Sqn from No 39 Maintenance Unit (MU) on 14 March 1942, but it did not remain on the squadron for long, however, being issued to No 315 'Polish' Sqn on 13 May. It was damaged as a result of operations that same day, and written off on 23 May.

12
Spitfire VC AB170 of Plt Off Jean Maridor, No 91 Sqn, Hawkinge, May 1942

Jean Maridor (3 and 1 shared destroyed, 2 probables, 3 damaged and 5 and 2 shared V1s destroyed) joined No 91 Sqn on 14 February 1942. He was flying AB170 on 23 May 1942 when he shot down the Spitfire VB of Flt Lt D G Molloy of No 402 'Canadian' Sqn in error. The Frenchman went on to make several legitimate claims, and was still serving on the squadron when he was killed attacking a V1 on 3 August 1944. AB170 was issued new to No 91 Sqn from No 39 MU on 13 March 1942. It was damaged following operations on 15 April and again on 23 May, when Maridor carried out a forced-landing at Hawkinge following his engagement with the Canadians – Molloy's wingman succeeded in badly damaging AB170 just moments after Maridor had shot his leader down. Following repairs (and the installation of a Merlin 46) at Air Service Training Ltd, the aircraft was used by Nos 610 and 611 Sqns, de Havilland and the Central Gunnery School, before being Struck off Charge on 8 November 1945.

13

Spitfire VI (serial unknown) of Plt Off Jean Maridor, No 91 Sqn, Hawkinge, August 1942

Jean Maridor rejoined the squadron on 12 August, having recovered from wounds sustained on 23 May. His first flights upon his return were local sorties, four of which were flown in 'DL-Z' – one of the unpopular Spitfire VIs. Although the serial number of this fighter is not recorded, the squadron used only seven Mk VIs, and two had been reissued to other units prior to 14 August. Therefore, this aircraft was either AB527, BR304, BR318, BR326 or BR585.

14

Spitfire VB R7292 NEWBURY I/CAROL OR – of Flt Lt Alan Andrews, No 91 Sqn, Hawkinge, September 1942

Alan Andrews (1 and 1 shared destroyed, 1 probable and 1 damaged) joined No 91 Sqn in 1941, and was OC 'B' Flight at the time of his death on 2 November 1942. R7292 was originally issued to No 71 'Eagle' Sqn on 26 August 1941, and was severely damaged on 1 October 1941. Rebuilt by Air Service Training Ltd and allocated to the newly-arrived 308th FS of the fledgling Eighth Air Force in June 1942, R7292 was passed on to No 91 Sqn in September. Flt Lt Andrews first flew the aircraft on the 15th of that month, and thereafter adopted it as his personal mount. It was damaged on 14 October and again 12 days later, when he was attacked by two Fw 190s. Repaired 'in the field' at Hawkinge, R7292 remained with the squadron until 21 March 1943, when it went to No 1 Civilian Repair Unit. Following rectification, and fuel system and wing modifications at Vickers, the aircraft was issued to No 306 'Polish' Sqn in late October 1943, followed by No 345 'French' Sqn in July 1944. R7292 was finally Struck off Charge on 8 December 1944 following a collision with Spitfire VB AB254 of No 308 'Polish' Sqn at Hawkinge on 2 November.

15

Spitfire LF VB BL527 of Plt Off Jean Maridor, No 91 Sqn, Hawkinge, October 1942

BL527 was Jean Maridor's personal aircraft (hence the Free French Cross of Lorraine), and he first flew it upon his return to the squadron from hospital on 13 August 1942. Thereafter, it appeared regularly in his log book until the fighter was damaged in an accident at Lympne on 21 October. Prior to this, Maridor had used it to probably destroy a Ju 88 on 7 September and strafe a minesweeper (with Flt Lt Andrews) off Berck on 6 October. BL527 had been issued to No 91 Sqn on 24 May 1942, having already seen service with Nos 134 and 81 Sqns. Following the accident on 21 October, the fighter was repaired at Westland Aircraft Ltd and then sent to Vickers-Armstrongs

for conversion into a Seafire IB (serial number PA100). It was issued to the Fleet Air Arm's 842 NAS in mid-1943, and subsequently served with the unit aboard the aircraft carrier HMS Fencer.

16

Spitfire LF VB BM543 of Flt Lt Geoff Pannell, No 91 Sqn, Lympne, December 1942

New Zealander Geoff Pannell (3 destroyed and 1 damaged) originally joined No 91 Sqn on 16 July 1941 as a sergeant pilot. A Battle of Britain veteran with No 3 Sqn, he arrived at Hawkinge from No 41 Sqn, and was commissioned in August that same year. Briefly seconded to No 111 Sqn for six weeks, Pannell eventually returned on 7 October, and went on to make several claims – Kenneth Wynn's volume A Clasp for 'The Few' lists his score as 5 destroyed, 4 probables and 5 damaged, but these claims cannot be officially verified. On 2 February 1942 Pannell was promoted to flight lieutenant and given command of 'A' Flight. He remained in this post until 20 April, when he went to Morris Motors as a test pilot, flying rebuilt Spitfires and newly-built Tiger Moths and Masters. Pannell returned for his third tour with the squadron on 16 September 1942, once again commanding 'A' Flight, before finally leaving on 12 July 1943. Pannell's BM543 was issued to No 91 Sqn on 15 June 1942, and it sustained damage following operations exactly one week later. Remaining with the squadron until 26 April 1943, the fighter was reissued to No 132 Sqn, and subsequently to Nos 122 and 234 Sqns. BM543 was slightly damaged in a flying accident on 16 October 1943, and was then sent to Morris Motors for major repair work on 16 January 1944 after a more serious incident. It was finally Struck off Charge on 20 October 1945, having also served with No 350 'Belgian' Sqn and the Central Gunnery School.

17

Spitfire LF VB AD261 of Flg Off Ron Batten, No 91 Sqn, Hawkinge, February 1943

Ron Batten joined No 91 Sqn in 1942, and served with the unit until he crash-landed in this specially-modified Spitfire in France after engaging a Do 217 over the Channel on 9 February 1943. Spending the remainder of the war as a PoW, he had claimed a solitary kill prior to his capture. AD261 had originally been issued to No 411 'Canadian' Sqn on 10 October 1941, and was then passed on to No 91 Sqn, via Air Service Training, on 18 April 1942. Modified to LF VB standard by Vickers-Amrstongs in August 1942, the fighter was returned to No 91 Sqn and fitted with an F24 oblique camera. AD261 subsequently completed a series of photo-reconnaissance operations over French ports before crash-landing with engine trouble on 9 February 1943. By then it had flown 325.35 hours in a busy career, which had also seen the fighter used by Sqn Ldr Harries to destroy a 'Bf 109F' (almost certainly a G-model) south of Pevensey on 20 January 1943 – he also damaged a second Messerschmitt and a Fw 190 during the same sortie.

18

Spitfire LF VB (serial unknown) of Sgt John Watterson, No 91 Sqn, Hawkinge, March 1943

'Wattie' Watterson (1 and 1 shared destroyed) was posted to No 91 Sqn as a sergeant pilot on 25 February 1943. Commissioned on 4 August that same year, he remained with the squadron until 8 January 1944, when he was posted for a rest at an OTU.

19

Spitfire F XII EN625 of Sqn Ldr Ray Harries, OC No 91 Sqn, Hawkinge, May 1943

Ray Harries (15 and 3 shared destroyed, 2 probables, 5 and 1 shared damaged and 1 V1 destroyed) joined No 91 Sqn as its CO on 8 December 1942. He was flying EN625 on 25 May 1943 when he destroyed two Fw 190s, and he went on to make several further claims before being promoted to command the Tangmere Wing on 19 August 1943. The fighter was issued to No 91 Sqn on 13 May 1943, and it remained with the unit until No 91 Sqn had fully converted to F XIVs on 9 March 1944. During its time with the 'Nigeria' Squadron, EN625 was frequently used by Flg Off Ray Nash, who was flying it on 16 June 1943 when he destroyed an Fw 190, and again on 20 October that same year when he downed a Bf 109G. Following a period in storage, the aircraft was used by No 451 'Australian' Sqn, the Fighter Leaders' School and the AFDU, before it was lost in a forced-landing in Norfolk on 11 December 1944.

20

Spitfire F XII MB832 of Flg Off Jean Maridor, No 91 Sqn, Hawkinge, May 1943

Jean Maridor first flew MB832 (a late-build F XII with a retractable tailwheel, seen here also fitted with a centrally-mounted slipper tank) on an Air Test on 22 May 1943. Three days later he used the fighter to destroy an Fw 190 off Folkestone, and he continued flying it until it was seriously damaged on 6 June 1943 (see photo on page 90). MB832 had only been issued to No 91 Sqn from the production line at High Post Aerodrome exactly three weeks earlier. Sent to Air Service Training for a total rebuild, it did not return to the squadron until 3 January 1944. This time it lasted only 20 days, being lost on the 23rd when Flt Sgt J H Hymas was downed by fighters on Ramrod 472. MB832 had flown for just 28.30 hours.

21

Spitfire F XII MB830 of Flt Lt Ian Matthew, No 91 Sqn, Hawkinge, May 1943

Ian Matthew was already serving on No 91 Sqn as a pilot officer when he was promoted to flying officer on 18 December 1942, replacing Flt Lt R C Brown as OC 'B' Flight in the process. He was awarded the DFC on 24 July 1943, and went on to take command of No 41 Sqn on 2 December 1943. MB830 was issued to No 91 Sqn on 17 May 1943, and was flown almost exclusively by Flt Lt Matthew until it was damaged on operations on 2 September 1943. Having been repaired, the aircraft was reissued to No 41 Sqn and duly written off in a forced-landing following engine failure on 23 June 1944.

22

Spitfire F XII MB836 of Flt Sgt Fred Lewis, No 91 Sqn, Tangmere, February 1944

Fred Lewis (1 damaged and 2 V1s destroyed) joined No 91 Sqn in January 1944, was commissioned in May and remained with the squadron until September 1945. MB836 was originally issued to No 91 Sqn on 22 August 1943, and was frequently flown by Lewis, as well as Tangmere Wing Leader, Wg Cdr Ray Harries. Indeed, the 'wingco' was flying it on 22 September 1943 when he destroyed an Fw 190, and again on 20 October when he 'bagged' two Bf 109Gs. The aircraft was also used by Flg Off 'Shag' O'Shaughnessy to down an Fw 190 on 26 September 1943. MB836 was returned to No 33 MU on 20 March 1944 and stored until issued to the Fighter Leaders' School on 28 September 1944. It was Struck off Charge on 16 May 1946.

23

Spitfire F XIV RM617 of Flg Off Jacques Andrieux, No 91 Sqn, West Malling, May 1944

'Jaco' Andrieux (6 destroyed, 4 probables and 2 damaged) joined No 91 Sqn on 6 July 1943, and he remained with the unit until posted to No 341 'French' Sqn on 17 June 1944. RM617 was frequently flown on operations by Flg Off Andrieux in May and early June 1944, this combination completing several successful Rhubarbs against enemy trucks and trains. Wt Off 'Red' Blumer returned to the squadron on 8 June, and flew RM617 for the first time six days later on a fighter sweep of Rouen and Evreux. He was subsequently killed when the aircraft crashed at Nettlestead, in Kent, during a nocturnal 'Diver' patrol on 25 June. RM617 had been issued to No 91 Sqn from No 39 MU on 1 May 1944, and three V1s had been destroyed by its various pilots (Flt Lt Bruce Moffett on 16 June, Flt Lt John Draper on the 19th and a shared claim by Flg Off Johnny Faulkner on the 19th) prior to its demise.

24

Spitfire F XIV NH698 of Flg Off Ken Collier, No 91 Sqn, West Malling, June 1944

Australian Ken Collier (7 V1s destroyed) joined No 91 Sqn on 23 February 1944. On 23 June 1944 he was flying NH698 when he became to first pilot to 'tip' a V1 using the wing of his aircraft. He was still serving with the squadron at the time of his death on 5 December 1944 during Ramrod 1394. NH698 had been issued to No 91 Sqn on 7 March 1944, and it was used extensively during the 'Diver' campaign, with claims being made by Flg Off Colin Ettles (1), Flg Off 'Mac' McPhie (1), Flt Lt Maridor (1) and Flg Off Ted Topham (1). Following service with No 91 Sqn, and probably a period in storage, the aircraft was issued to No 350 'Belgian' Sqn on 1 March 1945 and damaged on 9 April. After repair at Air Service Training, it was stored for nearly five years before being sold to Vickers-Armstrongs, who in turn supplied it to the Royal Thai Air Force (RTAF) as U14-10/93 in May 1950.

25

Spitfire F XIV RB169 of Flt Lt Ray Nash, No 91 Sqn, West Malling, July 1944

Ray Nash (2 and 1 shared destroyed and 17 and 3 shared V1s destroyed) joined No 91 Sqn on 16 September 1942, and remained with the unit until 21 November 1944, when he was posted to No 61 OTU for a rest. RB169 was his personal aircraft in the spring and summer of 1944, and he claimed 14 of his 20 V1s with it. Issued to No 91 Sqn on 29 February 1944, it was returned to de Havilland for modifications on 26 April. Once back with No 91 Sqn, RB169 was extensively used during the 'Diver' campaign, with claims being made by Flt Lt Nash and Flg Off Ted Topham (1). The aircraft was passed on to No 130 Sqn on 29 August 1944, and subsequently to No 350 'Belgian' Sqn, the Central Fighter Establishment and No 612 Sqn. It was

Struck off Charge on 26 August 1948 following a ground accident on 22 July.

26

Spitfire F XIV RB185 of Sqn Ldr Norman Kynaston, OC No 91 Sqn, West Malling, July 1944

Norman Kynaston (4 and 1 shared destroyed, 1 probable, 1 damaged and 22 V1s destroyed) joined No 91 Sqn on 18 November 1942 and was given command of the unit on 19 August 1943 – he was still CO at the time of his death, on 15 August 1944. RB185 was Kynaston's personal aircraft, and 13 of his 22 V1 claims were made whilst flying it. The fighter had been issued to No 91 Sqn on 12 March 1944, but was returned to Air Service Training for modifications in April. Once back in the frontline, RB185 was principly flown by Sqn Ldr Kynaston during the 'Diver' campaign, before being returned to storage on 24 July 1944. The aircraft remained inactive until 22 February 1945, when it was issued to No 350 'Belgian' Sqn. RB185 was still serving with the unit when it crash-landed near Cloppenburg, in Germany, on 5 April after being damaged by flak and then attacked by the Fw 190D of 5./JG 26's Unteroffizier Friedrich Rohrmann. The latter pilot was in turn downed minutes later by a second No 350 Sqn F XIV. RB185's pilot, Flg Off A Cresswell-Turner, had been flying an armed recce at the time, and after escaping the crash with minor wounds, he was quickly made a PoW.

27

Spitfire F XIV RB188 *BRÜMHILDE* of Flt Lt 'Johnny' Johnson, No 91 Sqn, West Malling, July 1944

'Johnny' Johnson (13 and 1 shared V1s destroyed) joined No 91 Sqn in 1942, and remained with the unit until 1946. RB188 was his personal aircraft, and five of his fourteen V1 claims were made whilst flying it. The fighter had been issued to No 91 Sqn on 29 February 1944, but was returned to Air Service Training for modifications on 5 May. Once back with No 91 Sqn, it was extensively used during the 'Diver' campaign largely by Flt Lt Johnson, although claims were also made by Flt Sgt Geoff Kay (1 shared), Flg Off Ken Collier (1) and Flt Flt Jean Maridor (1). Leaving No 91 Sqn on 9 August 1944, RB188 was issued firstly to No 130 Sqn and then No 350 Sqn. On 11 February 1945 it crashed in poor weather near Turnhouse, killing the pilot, Flt Sgt Ritchie. Repaired at Air Service Training, RB188 was sold to Vickers-Armstrongs on 10 May 1950, who subsequently supplied it to the RTAF as U14-18/93.

28

Spitfire F XIV RM656 of Flt Lt Jean Maridor, No 91 Sqn, Deanland, July 1944

RM656 was Air Tested by Jean Maridor on 15 July and then used extensively by him during the 'Diver' campaign. Although he flew at least 14 patrols in the aircraft, only one of his seven claims was made whilst flying it – the one that killed him, and destroyed the aircraft, on 3 August. Issued to No 91 Sqn on 14 July, RM656 replaced NH698 as 'DL-F'. Aside from Maridor's solitary claim, 'Paddy' Schade (1) and Norman Kynaston (4) also downed V1s with it.

29

Spitfire LF IX MK734 of Plt Off Fred Lewis, No 91 Sqn, Deanland, August 1944

Fred Lewis returned to No 91 Sqn on 14 August 1944,

having been commissioned. His first flight in an LF IX was on that day in MK734, which he subsequently flew a further six times. Lewis had always tried to fly the Spitfire coded 'DL-J' during his previous tour, and these included F XIVs RB177 and RM734. His usual LF IX was MJ822/ 'DL-J', which he flew throughout the autumn of 1944. Initially issued to No 56 Sqn, MK734 had been involved in a taxying collision with NH152 at Newchurch ALG on 21 May 1944. Following repair, it was sent to No 402 'Canadian' Sqn on 17 July, and then to No 91 Sqn on 9 August 1944. The aircraft was damaged again on 15 March 1945, and re-issued to No 326 'French' Sqn, before being transferred to the *Armée de l'Air* post-war.

30

Spitfire LF IX NH356 of Sqn Ldr Peter Bond, OC No 91 Sqn, Manston, December 1944

Peter Bond (7 and 3 shared V1s destroyed) arrived on No 91 Sqn on 5 February 1944 as a supernumerary squadron leader. He assumed command of the unit on 15 August 1944 after the death of Sqn Ldr Kynaston, and remained in the post until 1 March 1945. He was killed, as a wing commander, on 30 September 1946 in a Hornet F 1 when he flew into a hill in Wales in cloud. Issued new to No 91 Sqn on 30 August 1944, LF IX NH356 was duly passed on to No 1 Sqn and written off on 19 April 1945.

31

Spitfire LF IX ML341 of Flt Lt John Draper, No 91 Sqn, Manston, February 1945

John Draper (4 and 1 shared, 2 probables, 1 damaged and 6 V1s destroyed) was posted to No 91 Sqn on 14 June 1944, and served with the unit until June 1945, when he returned home to Canada. He was flying ML341 on 28 February 1945 (on Ramrod 1475) when he force-landed soon after take-off. The fighter ploughed through a hedge, which ripped its wings off, before coming to rest upside down. Fortunately, the pilot was not seriously injured. ML341 had initially been issued to No 56 Sqn on 10 May 1944, and then passed on to No 402 'Canadian' Sqn on 17 July. No 91 Sqn exchanged an F XIV for it on 9 August, and retained the fighter until it was written off by John Draper.

32

Spitfire F 21 LA234 of Flt Lt Roy Cruickshank, No 91 Sqn, Ludham, April 1945

Roy Cruickshank (10 and 1 shared V1s destroyed) joined No 91 Sqn in 1944, and remained with the unit until he was posted home to Canada on 6 June 1945. On 10 April 1945, he and Flg Off Johnny Faulkner were flying the unit's first F 21 operation when they were both shot down by flak – the pilots bailed out into the sea, and were both rescued unhurt. LA234, which had been issued to No 91 Sqn from No 33 MU on 9 March 1945, was the aircraft in which Flt Lt Cruickshank was shot down off Den Helder.

33

Spitfire F 21 LA200 of Plt Off Geoff Kay, No 91 Sqn, Ludham, May 1945

Geoff Kay (1 and 2 shared V1s destroyed) joined No 91 Sqn in 1944, and served with it until he crashed to his death on 12 May 1945 in F 21 LA200 whilst practising aerobatics over Ludham. This aircraft had been issued to No 91 Sqn from No 39 MU in early 1945.

INDEX

References to illustrations are shown in **bold**.
Plates are shown with page and caption locators in brackets.